"There is nothing soft or sentimental about the comfort offered in this book. Instead, it opens our eyes to see the miseries of our self-absorption and self-effort salvation and then applies the substantive, solid comfort of abundant grace, imputed righteousness, purchased peace, blessed wretchedness, no condemnation, no separation."

Nancy Guthrie, author of *Hearing Jesus Speak into Your Sorrow* and the Seeing Jesus in the Old Testament Bible study series

"Elyse's gratitude for God's grace spills out onto every page of this book as she opens the pages of her life and comforts us with the comfort she has received from God's Word. Her theological precision and her joy in God's extravagant love instructed my mind and thrilled my heart."

Susan Hunt, Women's Ministry Consultant, Christian Education and Publications, Presbyterian Church in America; author, *Spiritual Mothering*

"Martin Luther called Paul's letter to the Romans 'the most important piece in the New Testament. . . . It is purest Gospel.' My dear friend Elyse captures the purity and power of Romans here. In bite-size, digestible chunks she devotionally and practically unpacks the 'now-power' of the gospel, showing that the gospel doesn't simply free us from the past and free us for the future. It also frees us in the present from being enslaved to things like fear, insecurity, anger, self-reliance, bitterness, entitlement, and insignificance. Being both a seasoned counselor and a top-notch theologian, I can't think of anyone better to comfort sinners through Romans than Elyse!"

Tullian Tchividjian, Pastor, Coral Ridge Presbyterian Church; author, *Glorious Ruin*

COMFORTS
FROM ROMANS

Other Crossway Books by Elyse Fitzpatrick:

Give Them Grace: Dazzling Your Kids with the Love of Jesus, coauthor (2011)

Counsel from the Cross: Connecting Broken People to the Love of Christ, coauthor (2009)

Comforts from the Cross: Celebrating the Gospel One Day at a Time (2009)

Because He Loves Me: How Christ Transforms Our Daily Life (2008)

COMFORTS FROM ROMANS

Celebrating the Gospel One Day at a Time

ELYSE M. FITZPATRICK

 CROSSWAY

WHEATON, ILLINOIS

Comforts from Romans: Celebrating the Gospel One Day at a Time

Copyright © 2013 by Elyse M. Fitzpatrick

Published by Crossway
      1300 Crescent Street
      Wheaton, Illinois 60187

Cover design: Connie Gabbert

First printing 2013

Printed in the United States of America

Unless otherwise indicated, Scripture quotations are from the ESV® Bible (*The Holy Bible, English Standard Version*®), copyright © 2001 by Crossway. 2011 Text Edition. Used by permission. All rights reserved.

Scripture quotations marked HCSB have been taken from *The Holman Christian Standard Bible*®. Copyright © 1999, 2000, 2002, 2003 by Holman Bible Publishers. Used by permission.

All emphases in Scripture quotations have been added by the author.

Trade paperback ISBN: 978-1-4335-3319-8
PDF ISBN: 978-1-4335-3320-4
Mobipocket ISBN: 978-1-4335-3321-1
ePub ISBN: 978-1-4335-3322-8

Library of Congress Cataloging-in-Publication Data

Fitzpatrick, Elyse, 1950-
   Comforts from Romans : celebrating the Gospel one day
     at a time / Elyse M. Fitzpatrick.
     p. cm.
   ISBN 978-1-4335-3319-8
   1. Bible N.T. Romans—Textbooks. I. Title.
BS2665.55.F58   2013
227'.106—dc23   2012027061

Crossway is a publishing ministry of Good News Publishers.

VP		23	22	21	20	19	18	17	16	15	14	13
15	14	13	12	11	10	9	8	7	6	5	4	3	2	1

To
John Sale and David Wojnicki

Thank you for loving Phil and me
And for loving our church

Contents

INTRODUCTION

Martin Luther called the book of Romans

> the chief part of the New Testament and the very purest Gospel, and is worthy not only that every Christian should know it word for word, by heart, but occupy himself with it every day, as the daily bread of the soul. It can never be read or pondered too much, and the more it is dealt with the more precious it becomes, and the better it tastes.[1]

Ponder those words. Luther said that our hearts should be occupied with the truths contained within the book of Romans "every day." In fact, he said that it is such an important book that it should be to us like "daily bread of the soul." My soul needs that *daily* bread because although I go to bed at night believing the gospel, I wake up every morning needing to hear it again. Sure, Jesus loves me. Sure, the gospel is good news. But why did my coffee pot have to overflow today, when I'm already in such a hurry?

I know I should feast on the Bread of Life every morning. But I don't. Some mornings I have to run out the door before I've breakfasted on him. Other mornings I dither away my time, messing about on Facebook or answering e-mails, and then I realize that a good part of the morning is gone and I still haven't sat down with him.

My guess is that it may be the same for you. The demands of family, friends, and work, the siren call of the Internet, a relentless and futile curiosity about "what's going on," all draw me away from the repast my soul needs. Other times it's just a beautiful day and I want to go to the beach or the pool or the park or anywhere just so that I'm doing something fun!

And so I run out the door hungry. I don't always remember (or even want to remember) to feast on this Bread. Other times I'll admit that I'm just not that hungry, at least not for him. And then, inevitably, I end up at the same place every time: working or buying or playing or clicking more, despairing when I realize that I've tried to fill my soul with something other than him, and all my work or efforts to distract or fill or satisfy myself are not enough to do anything other than leave me starving for more. Oh, for a quieted heart that would simply sit down at his feet and let him feed me every day!

Hence this book. It's my prayer that this book will do three things for us all. First, I pray that it will make us really hungry for the Bread of Life (John 6:35). Second, I pray that the Spirit will use it to nourish our souls on the gospel. And more than anything else, I pray that this little devotional will draw us toward the book of Romans itself and, of course, ultimately, to the great love of God our Father and to the boundless love and incomprehensible labor of our Lord and Savior, Jesus Christ.

So, here's what I suggest: first, I recommend that you begin reading through Romans. Because this little book is not meant to be a commentary on the entire book of Romans but rather a devotional taste of the truths presented in chapters 1 through 8, you could determine to read at the least the particular chapter in Romans I'm referencing so that you'll understand what I'm saying in the context of Paul's thought. If you have Internet capability, my suggestion is that you listen to it online at a website such as this one for the English Standard Version of the Bible (ESV): http://esvbible.org/search/romans. Reading while you listen is probably the best way to begin to understand, and I personally find it a great help in corralling my distracted thoughts. Of course, you could also read it out loud to yourself.

As I said above, my goal in this book is to make us hungry for him and to begin to present Christ to us in such a way that we will taste and see that he is good. I admit that I have chosen very specific passages from Romans to accomplish this goal. I have not commented on everything Paul presents in Romans, nor have I tried to exegete entire chapters. There are wonderful study books already in the marketplace on this topic,[2] not the least of which is Luther's commentary on Romans (especially his *Preface to Romans*, which was written in the later years of his life after his theological thought had matured).

You'll see that I've worked a lot in some portions of Romans and only pulled a passage or two out of other ones. Again, I'm not trying to exegete the whole book but rather cull from the book one message: the absolutely shocking message of grace.

I hope that this devotional will create a hunger for more of Romans because, as Luther writes, it is "the very purest Gospel," and whether or not we realize it, the message of the gospel is the message we need to hear. There are so many anti-gospel messages being proclaimed today in our churches, self-help messages about how to work harder and discover your potential and make Jesus proud. All these messages are anti-gospel because they're about you, your work, your goodness, your plans and success, and, yes, even your obedience. They bend you in on yourself. They make you think that everything is up to you and that your performance is all that matters. And they don't train your palate to savor the sweet, humble manna from above. Rather than bending you in on yourself, Paul doesn't even mention your obligations until Romans 6, where he simply tells you to consider what Christ has already done. *You are not the subject of Romans.* He is, and that's how it should be.

Luther wrote that the message of the gospel articulated in Romans can "never be read or pondered too much." We never have to worry about becoming bored with it, as if the gospel were some new fad that will fade into obscurity like some one-hit wonder. Our souls will never grow tired of the old, old story, simply because it is the job of the Holy Spirit to make Jesus Christ freshly delicious to us. I'm convinced that even in heaven, when faith has become sight, when we have perfect faculties for thought, when our bodies are finally able to persevere through weakness, tiredness, and distraction, even then, we won't be able to fully plumb the magnificent truths presented in Paul's letter to Rome and embodied before us. Bored? A flash in the pan? The gospel? Hardly! The truth is that, as Luther writes, "the more it is dealt with the more precious it becomes, and the better it tastes." So, scoot yourself on up to the table and ask the Spirit to absolutely glut you with the gospel from Romans. Is your mouth watering? Oh, I hope so.

Day 1

A Ruined Righteousness

Paul, a servant of Christ Jesus . . . —Romans 1:1

The great apostle Paul, who wrote much of the New Testament, established churches, and ultimately suffered martyrdom, didn't deserve God's blessing. He didn't deserve to call himself a "servant," a "bondservant," or even a "love slave" of Jesus Christ. No, he deserved to be called an "enemy" because, after all, that's the identity he had chosen for himself. You remember that before he became Christ's servant, he was a man who breathed out "threats and murder" against Christ's church (Acts 9:1). A servant of Christ Jesus? Hardly.

Paul gloried in his role as persecutor of the church, because he hated the gospel. Yes, I know: "hated" seems like a strong word, but that is exactly how Paul felt. He hated the gospel so much that he determined to root it out and ruin the lives of those who loved it (Gal. 1:13). But then God ruined him, not by giving him the judgment he deserved but by giving him grace instead.

Don't be mistaken. Aside from his hatred of Christians, Paul would have been just the sort of person you would have wanted for a neighbor. He came from a good home; he always obeyed all the rules. He would have mowed his lawn and voted, and never would have hung around with shady characters. Yes, we would assume that Paul was a great candidate to receive the love of God. After all, who was more zealous for righteousness than he? But our assumption would have been wrong. Of course, God loved Paul but not because Paul was good. No, God loved Paul in spite of his religious goodness, which was the very thing that made Paul repulsive in God's eyes (Isa. 64:6). You see, Paul's problem was not that he was outwardly bad, but rather that he trusted in his own goodness and ability to satisfy the law's demands. It was his self-trust that made him the enemy of Jesus. And so one day, on the road to Damascus, God ruined his self-righteousness—*with grace.*

Here's the shocking news: God loves to display his mercy by wrecking "good" people. That seems counterintuitive, doesn't it? We think that God loves to wreck bad people, to strip them of their badness, and, of course, he does. But God also delights in wrecking those who seem good, at least outwardly. Paul's primary impediment to relationship with God was not his irreligion. It was his religion. Don't forget: Paul truthfully boasted that he had been "advancing" beyond all his contemporaries and was "extremely zealous" for the law (Gal. 1:14). Paul saw himself as a champion of the one true faith, and it was this very identity that barred him from serving the God he would have said he was living for. Paul needed wrecking, and Jesus was just the one to do it. So one day, just when we would assume that Paul had gone too far and really blown his chances with Jesus, Jesus knocked him off his feet, blinded him, and introduced him to grace. What a Savior!

Paul's story is good news for those of us who are tempted to put our trust in ourselves, in our own ability to work hard enough to merit God's favor. Grace is so surprising! It's surprising because while it may seem likely that a prostitute would recognize her need for rescue, the homeschooling, bread-baking, devotion-reading mom who attends her local church faithfully (while trusting in her own goodness) will choke on the humiliating message of gospel rescue. Rescue? Why would she need rescuing?

If we are to embrace the message of the gospel and become free, joyous, and zealous servants of Jesus Christ, then all—and I really mean *all*—the work has to be done by him. Why? *So that all the glory will go to him,* so that we boast in the work of Jesus *alone* (Isa. 48:11). "Then what becomes of our boasting?" Paul asks. "It is excluded," he answers (Rom. 3:27). Paul learned how the Father strips us of everything we're tempted to trust in. He confessed that he had finally given up relying on his own goodness and was instead counting all his religious goodness

> as loss because of the surpassing worth of knowing Christ Jesus my Lord. For his sake I have suffered the loss of all things and count them as rubbish, in order that I may gain Christ and be found in him, *not having a righteousness of my own* that comes from the law, but that which comes through faith in Christ, the righteousness from God that depends on faith. (Phil. 3:8–9)

Through the good news of the gospel, the Lord graciously strips us of our slavish devotion to our reputation and says, "Count it as rubbish so that you might gain the true righteousness from my Son." He frees us from the incessant nagging of our inner slave driver and frees us to love others without being slavishly driven by them either. He ruins our pride in our accomplishments, thereby freeing us from the demand that others live up to our expectations.

As our short time today now nears an end, I wonder how you would describe yourself. Do you think of yourself as God's servant? I would imagine that you do, but what does that servant identity rest on? Paul had formerly assumed that he was serving God because he was zealous and working harder than anyone else, and that perspective made him cruel and demanding. Paul was wrong. He was wrong because he trusted in himself instead of in Jesus. Does your servant identity rest primarily on the work you hope to accomplish today? Or does it rest on the service and righteousness of Another? Are you free to love others who do not live up to your standards? Can you say, "Nothing in my hands I bring, simply to Thy cross I cling"?

Day 2

THE GOSPEL OF GOD

Paul, a servant of Christ Jesus . . . set apart for the gospel of God.
—Romans 1:1

There are certain "Christian" words that we can become overly familiar with. Sadly, the word *gospel* is primary among them. After all, our Christian life doesn't even begin until we hear and believe the gospel; but then most of us go on, leaving it behind with the rest of the trappings of our spiritual infancy, as if we didn't need it anymore. My guess is that about now you might be wondering if you need to read this today. I mean, after all, don't you already know the gospel? Even the word itself seems trite, doesn't it? *Gospel*—really?

Believe me, I understand this response because it's how I respond too. My heart is so bent in upon itself that it's easy for me to think that I already get everything that needs to be gotten about the gospel and that I should move on to where the real action is, in other words, me and my day. Won't you please bear with me, though, while I rehearse gospel truth to you once again? Perhaps it's the very thing your tired old soul needs to hear today.

The word *gospel* literally means "good message" or "good news." In this case, it is a message or news report specifically about Jesus— who he is and what he has done. It is not a report about us or how we're doing. It is a report about how the Son, the second person of the Trinity, left heaven to be clothed with human flesh and become a human being, just like us. Jesus was born in the same way as the rest of us; he lived in a real home with real parents, siblings, and friends. Like you, he felt tired and hungry, and when the desert sun beat down on his head, he perspired and thirsted for a drink. He yawned and stretched, rubbed sore feet, felt the sting when his siblings hit him and friends deserted him. He enjoyed hugs from his mom and dad, a splash in cool water, and a good meal. He had to learn table manners and how to read. He grew in his understanding of his identity and calling, all the while perfectly fulfilling every command of the law in our place.

Then, after living in virtual obscurity for thirty years, he began his life's work of publicly inaugurating the kingdom of God: he called disciples, taught the masses, healed the sick, and delivered those who were oppressed by the Devil. He perfectly fulfilled his life's work as he prepared to give himself as an offering for sin. He suffered every day and especially during the final days of his earthly life. He cried in Gethsemane as he became more and more aware of God's impending wrath. Like a lamb, he stood silently before Pilate and the Sanhedrin. He was mocked, scourged, stripped, beaten, and spit upon. He bore the crossbeam up Calvary's hill and was hoisted up between heaven and earth. And then he began to suffer like no one had ever suffered before or would ever suffer again.

His Father poured down an eternity's worth of wrath upon him for all the sins of his chosen ones—in three hours. Then, when he had finished all his work, when he had emptied every drop from the cup of his Father's wrath, he relinquished his life into the hands of the Father he loved, who had just crushed him. His body was taken down and placed in a cave. A stone was rolled in front of the opening. All was darkness. But then, after three days, he was raised to new life by the power of the Holy Spirit. Again he emerged into the dim light of our world, bringing with him the ineffable brightness of a universe remade, having reversed the curse and defeated the power of darkness forever.

For the next forty days he taught his friends about the kingdom of God and gave them deep assurance of his resurrection. With great joy he then ascended to his home and was received into heaven's loving embrace. Gifts of celebration were sent back upon his church, gifts that would remind, preserve, enlighten, and empower his bride as he took up his throne, ruling as King over her until he is, at last, reunited with her. This is the good news of Jesus Christ; this is the gospel.

But the gospel also has a subjective component. It is the *good* news about what Jesus has done, but unlike any other news you might see on television, his work speaks to us personally. It is good news *for us*. The gospel brings us into relationship with him; it transforms and liberates us; it makes us altogether new. The facts about his incarnation, perfection, death, resurrection, ascension, rule, and bestowal of the Spirit change everything. His incarnation tells you that he knows by experience what it is to be you today. Are you walking through a time of trial? He's walked through it too. He understands completely. His death and perfect life mean that not only are you forgiven for your sin, that God has no wrath left for you, but also that his record of perfect obedience is yours—today.

The resurrection demonstrates that just as the power of death has been forever broken, the power of sin in your life has been crushed, too. It also speaks to God's acceptance of Jesus's sacrifice for you. His ascension tells you that the incarnation is ongoing: he continues to wear your flesh and rules from heaven with nail-scarred hands. By sending the Spirit, he assures us that the Father has welcomed him home and that we will be welcomed home one day also. Now, *that's good news!*

Oh, my friends, do you think about this good news every day? Won't you let it inform, enflame, embolden, and cheer you? The gospel? Oh, yeah. We should be like little children screaming, "Again! Again!" when we hear the gospel, and never let our calloused hearts grow tired of it. "Again! Again!"

Day 3

A Hidden Glory

*. . . concerning his Son, who was descended from David according
to the flesh and was declared to be the Son of God in power according to the Spirit of holiness by his resurrection from the dead, Jesus
Christ our Lord . . .* —Romans 1:3–4

The gospel is good news about Jesus Christ. Paul tells us that Jesus
was the expected one the prophets had foretold, the one the Law and
the Prophets bore witness to (Rom. 3:21; 16:26); he was Messiah,
David's son, who would reign eternally from his throne (Ps. 89:3–4;
Jer. 23:5–6). For hundreds of years the nation of Israel had been await-
ing the Messiah's coming, but many failed to recognize him when
he finally arrived. Why? *Because his glory was hidden in weakness
and humility.* He didn't look much like a king. Where were his royal
robes? Where was his bejeweled scepter? No one heard his voice in the
street demanding allegiance (Matt. 12:19). If he was Israel's king, why
wasn't he crushing her enemies under his boot instead of healing the
enemies' servants? (Matt. 8:5–13). Paul describes Jesus's humiliation
in Philippians 2:6–7:

> Though he was in the form of God, [he] did not count equality with
> God a thing to be grasped, but emptied himself, by taking the form
> of a servant, being born in the likeness of men.

Where was his glory? It was hidden in weakness and humiliation,
in questionable ancestry, in poverty and insignificance. Yes, Jesus
was the son of David, but not in the way you would expect. He was
descended from David "according to the flesh," not according to good
breeding, not according to sterling reputation or great political power,
but according to the flesh.

Think of that: Paul's first description of Jesus wasn't that he is the "Son of God in power," but rather that he "descended from David according to the flesh." What was David like? We like to clean him up and think of him as the sweet psalmist, a "man after God's own heart" (see 1 Sam. 13:14; Acts 13:22), and he was that. But he was also an adulterer and a murderer. He was responsible not only for the deaths of his illegitimate child and of Uriah (Bathsheba's husband), but also for the slaughter of seventy thousand others (2 Sam. 24:15). Jesus identified with David *according to the flesh*. He identified with David, the murderer, the sinner. He isn't ashamed to be called David's brother (Heb. 2:11).

Of course, that Jesus was "descended from David according to the flesh" means that he is incarnate, fully human, but it also means that Jesus shares our ancestry. He takes on our humiliation and shame. In order for Jesus to be our mediator, he had to suffer every part of our humiliation, to identify fully with us. He had to start out with a bad reputation—like us. Wasn't he the illegitimate son? Wasn't he the son of a loser? Didn't he hang out with losers?

For our sake, *Jesus had to be fully tempted to see his identity as rooted solely in his earthly reputation*. Then he had to fight to fulfill his purpose as the incarnate Son even *though his glory was (temporarily) hidden*. He had to suffer the humiliation of the thorns, the lash, the robe, the spikes, the insults, and the scoffing. And then he had to suffer the humiliation of being deserted by his Father just when his reputation should have, finally and at last, been fully proved. Instead, at that pivotal moment when he should have been vindicated, we hear him crying out in agony, "My God, my God, why have you forsaken me?" (Matt. 27:46; Mark 15:34).

Oh, now finally, this is the time for glory, but it comes *after* shame: he "was declared to be the Son of God in power according to the Spirit of holiness by his resurrection from the dead, Jesus Christ our Lord." For him, humiliation meant being called the Son of David *before* he was proven to be the Son of God with power. "The Gospel, then, is the joyous message of Christ, the Son of God, who first humbled Himself and then was glorified through the Holy Spirit."[3]

Ah, here's power and glory on display. But it doesn't come the way we think it will. It flows out of great weakness. In fact, it comes *because* of the great weakness, humility, and submission of Jesus. He would not have known the power of the resurrection, the majestic name "Son of God with power," if he had not first known the humiliation of death. "*Therefore* God has highly exalted him and bestowed on him the name that is above every name" (Phil. 2:9).

The gospel takes everything we think we know about getting ahead and turns it upside down. It shows us the power of weakness and the glory in humiliation. I admit that I hate humiliation. I don't like feeling weak, and in every way that I continue to try to hang on to my good reputation and fight against God's humbling, I militate against the gospel and the work of Jesus. I forget that God "resists the proud but gives grace to the humble" (1 Pet. 5:5; see also James 4:6). I always want the crown without the cross. Is it the same for you? The good news is that Jesus walked through humiliation perfectly so that even when we succumb to our pride, we have his good reputation—a reputation of sweet humility and perfect submission to God's will. We have his identity now: we are his royal sons, crowned with his glory and honor, or as Stuart Townend sings, "All the blessings he deserved [are] poured on my unworthy soul."[4]

Day 4

LOVED BY GOD

. . . including you who are called to belong to Jesus Christ, To all
those in Rome who are loved by God and called to be saints . . .
—Romans 1:6–7

On any given day, what thoughts float through your mind about who
you are and what God thinks of you? Do you ever think, "I hope
that I obey today so that God will love me"? Perhaps you don't say
those exact words; maybe what you feel is something more akin to an
uneasy sense that the Lord is just a tad irritated with you and waiting
for an opportunity to set you straight. Yes? You're not alone. As I've
spoken to Christians around the country—and observed the work-
ings of my own heart—it seems that rest in God's absolute love and
welcome doesn't come naturally to us.

It's interesting that Paul introduces his masterpiece on the gospel
with this thought: "You belong to Jesus Christ. You are loved by God.
You are saints." He begins by briefly introducing the Messiah, then
he describes his own identity, and then, finally, ours. Before he gets to
the whole world being guilty before God, before he speaks of double
imputation (Christ's righteousness for our sin) and how we should
respond, he tells us that we are loved by God and are his possession.
He tells us that we are his saints, his holy ones.

Why would Paul start here?

Of course, I don't know exactly why the Holy Spirit had Paul
write what he did but I can guess. Perhaps people in the Roman world
needed to hear that they were called, loved, and welcomed by God just
as much as we do. The ancient culture in which they lived was hyper-
religious, and terrible fears bred suspicions that at any point one might
offend some capricious god or fail to please an all-powerful emperor.
Disease, tragedy, and death lurked around every corner. There were

hundreds of gods—gods for every occurrence and difficulty, gods you had to appease or suffer the consequences. They were impetuous, angry, and jealous. In addition, their emperor, who claimed to be a god, was demanding, wicked, and cruel. The rules were constantly changing, life was out of control, without rhyme or reason, and while the gods seemed to help make it more manageable, in another way they made it more terrifying because you could never be sure that you might not be offending in some way.

Can you see why Paul might have started his letter as he did? The Roman Christians needed to know that their God wasn't like the gods of the culture that surrounded them. We need to know it too. At first blush it might seem that we're nothing like the ancient Romans, but aren't we? Did you ever see anyone knock on wood or throw salt over his shoulder or shudder when a black cat crossed her path? These are pagan constructs, fresh from Roman daily life. Even as Christians, in some ways we're just as superstitious as they were. We just run our superstitions through a religious grid. Did we have a flat tire on the way to work? It was probably because we didn't take time to do our devotions today. Did our washing machine overflow? Maybe God is irritated with us and trying to teach us a lesson. Do you ever say, "It's just going to be 'one of those days'"?

Christianity stands completely apart from all other religions because it's not up to us to work our way into our God's favor. We do worship a holy God who demands loving obedience, but he's unique because he took all the judgment for our failure onto himself. He's already done everything for us. This is the scandalous, incredible Christian message of the incarnate God becoming man and dying in our place to bring us to himself. And it's the message that we need to hear over and over again because we're never completely convinced of it. That's not to say that we don't believe it at all; it's just that there always seems to be some sort of lurking suspicion that he's not as good as he says he is. He declares his love for us in the most lavish manner, and still we wake up wondering if he'll like us better today if somehow we can get our act together.

Even so, he patiently continues to assure and reassure us of his love. He's already demonstrated it in the most outrageous way: "God shows his love for us in that while we were still sinners, Christ died for us" (Rom. 5:8). He absolutely delights in demonstrating his mercy and love. Rather than our failures frustrating him, our sin simply serves to make his mercy more beautiful.[5] We can believe in this love and rest in it, or we can try to figure out what makes him tick and then make a list of rules we need to obey to keep him from punishing us. Either we can believe in his love and welcome, or we can move back to ancient Rome in our hearts.

What do you have to do to be a recipient of this kind of love? Simply believe. Believe that it is true. Don't worry: you don't even have to remember it perfectly to continue to be a recipient of it. Why? Because Jesus always remembered it perfectly in your place. He's given us grace and peace, not superstitions and lists. We are loved by God, and we live in his world—not in a world of fate or luck or karma. Oh, glorious, shocking, transforming truth! We are loved by God! We belong to him! No superstitions, no lists, no getting our act together to make him love us. Simply believe.

Day 5

THE RIGHTEOUSNESS
OF GOD

*For I am not ashamed of the gospel, for it is the power of God
for salvation to everyone who believes, to the Jew first and also
to the Greek. For in it the righteousness of God is revealed from
faith for faith, as it is written, "The righteous shall live by faith."*
—Romans 1:16–17

How much righteousness do you need to be saved? How much law
do you have to obey in order to gain salvation? Will good intentions
or sincere efforts suffice? No, good intentions and sincere efforts will
never be enough. *Absolute perfection at all times* is what is required.
Every person must fulfill every single law in the entire Bible at every
moment of every day of their life, no matter what their circumstances
or abilities. When Jesus said that our righteousness had to exceed that
of the scribes and Pharisees (Matt. 5:20), he wasn't using hyperbole.
He said, "You must therefore be *perfect* as your heavenly Father is
perfect" (Matt. 5:48).

Oh, and by the way, it's not just an outward obedience that's
required. No, the only acceptable obedience is one that comes from
the heart, with the sole motivation being pure love for God and neighbor. This kind of obedience is not about feeling better about yourself
or doing unto others so they will return the favor. Jesus summarized
God's requirements in this way: "You shall love the Lord your God
with all your heart and with all your soul, and with all your mind. . . .
And you shall love your neighbor as yourself" (Matt. 22:37–39). All of
our righteousness is tethered to our loving God and man perfectly—
and none of us does.

In light of these truths, the difficulty that is before every person is
this: *How am I going to obey and gain life and salvation? Am I going*

to rely on my ability or on the ability of Another? That's not just a question for unbelievers. It's a question for believers, too. You may have been saved thirty years ago, but you still need to answer that question every day. Upon whom does your salvation, your welcome, your adoption, and your forgiveness rest?

Believers need a powerful reminder of the answer to this question because in our heart of hearts we know that even though we are saved, we're not making the grade. The incessant demand for perfection continues to plague us. While at heart we know there's no excuse for our selfishness and self-centeredness, for our unbelief and idolatry, year after year we fail to live up to the demands of our conscience and God's law. So we numb ourselves through some sort of self-indulgence or determine that, by golly, this year we're going to do better. Maybe we'll even get really serious and buy one of the hundreds of "How to Get Your Act Together" books churned out every year (thin pabulum for our guilty, enslaved conscience) only to find that at year's end, we remain weak, despairing, and fatally flawed.

Oh, is there any hope for us? Our hearts echo Paul's cry, "Wretched man that I am! Who will deliver me from this body of death?" (Rom. 7:24). Is there any power that can free us from the law's demand and our failure? Is there any salvation, any way to breathe without transgressing the Lord's requirements? Oh, yes, and thank God! The answer from heaven is the powerful remedy. It is a resounding yes that shatters all our fears and insecurities. It frees and assures us; it delights and empowers us. And it is the only voice with enough weight to silence every accusation once and for all. What is that answer? The gospel, of course.

The gospel is the power of God for our salvation. It is the good news that the "righteousness of God" has been lived out in the person and work of Jesus Christ and that, if we believe, this perfect righteousness and record is ours—*just as it was his.* Think of that! Salvation is ours because Jesus fulfilled every demand of the law from a heart of perfect love, beginning with Bethlehem's ignominious cries all through Calvary's scandalous death. Salvation is ours because God has determined to provide it for us. It was his power that brought it to pass—his power caused the incarnation; he "overshadowed" the Virgin Mary. It was his power that enabled the Son to live a life of perfect obedience, always doing the things that were pleasing to his Father. And it was his incalculable power that enabled him to pour out fury upon the soul of the Son he loved. Think of the power that it took for him to punish the righteous One! The gospel, not your works, goodness, or determination, is the power of God for salvation.

Ready to hear the good news again? In Christ the righteousness that God requires he powerfully gives to all who will believe! And belief in his utter satisfaction is the *only* power that can free us from shame, assure us of his welcome, and transform us. The gospel is the only good news powerful enough to cleanse and assure us.

So today the questions you must ask yourself are these: Who will you rely on to fulfill the law? How will you answer your conscience's demands? Will you rest in the righteousness of God bestowed on you simply because you believe, or will you determine to try harder so that you can approve of yourself and earn God's favor? If you believe, the righteousness of God is yours—now. Will you rest in his power alone?

Day 6

ACCORDING TO HIS WORKS

He will render to each one according to his works: to those who by patience in well-doing seek for glory and honor and immortality, he will give eternal life; but for those who are self-seeking and do not obey the truth, but obey unrighteousness, there will be wrath and fury. There will be tribulation and distress for every human being who does evil, the Jew first and also the Greek, but glory and honor and peace for everyone who does good, the Jew first and also the Greek. For God shows no partiality. —Romans 2:6–11

Let me ask you to go back and reread the verses with which I opened this day's reading. What do you see there? At first glance we see what appears to be a way to earn salvation. In fact, the verse does plainly say that by "patience in well-doing" and doing good one will gain glory, honor, peace, and immortality and earn eternal life. It also says that for those who are "self-seeking and do not obey the truth, but obey unrighteousness, there will be wrath and fury" and "tribulation and distress." Sounds like a recipe for working your way to heaven, right? But is that what it is?

This is one of those times when the context of a verse means everything. If we detach this passage from the rest of Romans (and the rest of the Bible), it can look like an encouragement toward works righteousness: Patiently Do Good: Earn Heaven. But, when we look at the passage in context, we see that Paul is simply continuing the argument that he began in chapter 1. In chapter 1, he declared that the gospel is the power of God for salvation, and then in verses 18–32 he goes on to show how the non-Jewish world had responded to the truth that nature taught them about God. Rather than acknowledging, honoring, and giving him thanks, "they exchanged the truth of God for a lie and worshiped and served the creature rather than the Creator" (v. 25). Paul's point? The Gentiles serve idols of their own design and therefore deserve "to die" (v. 32). He declares that the entire pagan world lies under the wrath and judgment of God.

Likewise, in chapter 2, Paul demolishes the self-righteousness of the religious person and the Jew. He begins by addressing their misguided reliance on their own works as a way to earn salvation, but he isn't commending them or encouraging them to try harder. Instead, he calls them hypocrites because they judge others who break God's laws and yet disobey the very same laws themselves (vv. 3, 21–22). "You who boast in the law dishonor God by breaking the law. For, as it is written, 'The name of God is blasphemed among the Gentiles because of you" (vv. 23–24). These aren't words meant to build self-esteem. They are words meant to drive us all to despair—and to the gospel. Remember that Paul's thesis statement is that the gospel is the power of God for salvation.

Romans 2:6–11 isn't meant to encourage us to rely on our own ability to obey either. Although it is true that *if* we were "patient in well-doing" and *if* we were to do "good," *then* God would reward us, we're actually in the same position as the Jew. We're all hypocritical law breakers, and we aren't earning glory, honor, and immortality. What are we earning? Wrath.

> But because of your hard and impenitent heart you are storing up wrath for yourself on the day of wrath when God's righteous judgment will be revealed. (v. 5)

Not even God's chosen people, the ones he called out to be a royal priesthood, a holy nation, a people for his own possession (Deut. 10:15; Ex. 19:6), could earn their way to heaven by their good works. And if they couldn't do it, neither can we. Rather, if anyone relies on his own work as a way to earn salvation, he will suffer God's wrath as a law breaker. Let's face it: it doesn't matter what your ancestry is or how diligently you work; there is no partiality with God. He won't reward anyone for anything less than perfection. There is only one way to earn glory, honor, immortality, peace, and eternal life. It's by being perfectly patient in completely righteous living, fulfilling all of God's law all of the time with a perfectly pure heart.

It doesn't take much discernment to see that if perfection is the requirement, we're all in serious trouble. Neither the idol-worshiping Gentile nor the self-righteous hypocrite can offer any response in defense against God's righteous judgment. Paul's "If you work hard enough, then I will reward you" model brings with it judgment rather than encouragement. Or does it? Is there a way for us to fulfill the obligations implicit in Paul's *if*/*then* proposition without denuding its demands or giving up in despair?

Yes, we can fulfill these obligations. You see, salvation *is* by works after all, *just not our works*. Salvation is by the works of Jesus Christ, who was patient in well-doing and earned "glory and honor and immortality," "eternal life," and "peace" for us. For thirty-three years he was perfectly patient in well-doing, earning a perfect record for us. Then, on Calvary he received the "wrath and fury" and "tribulation and distress" we deserve. He died in our place, as one who was "self-seeking" and did not "obey the truth" but was rather "unrighteous" and "evil." He received in his person all God's wrath and fury for all our sin and wickedness. He died the death we deserve at the hands of the Father, who loves him and would have delighted in bestowing upon him the glory, honor, and immortality he had earned.

What then shall we do to live in the light of his reward? We must die to our chronic self-assurance and pride. He earned it all. He paid it all. We simply believe—period. It's the only way. We must take up our cross and die to our pride and hope of being good enough to earn God's blessings. We have to throw our lot in with him, in his death *completely*. And we have to plunge ourselves into his perfect law keeping, vindicating resurrection, and atoning work *every day*. We have to die to our desire to approve of our record and earn something from God and then identify entirely with him—with his sinless life, substitutionary death, and bodily resurrection *as our only hope*. And then, on the days when we forget that our hope of attaining some sort of blessing-earning goodness was openly annihilated by God two thousand years ago, we go back and remember again and again. What is our work? How can we earn blessing? We die to ourselves and live to Christ.

Today, if we simply believe that his righteousness and death are sufficient, we walk in the new life that he has earned for us. We have the glory, honor, immortality, eternal life, and peace he earned so that we are now free to live and to die, to patiently do good, to repent when we fail, to be zealous for good work, and to hope in God's blessing on our lives because all that self-focused, glory-chasing self-righteousness has been done away with. We've been given the glory, honor, immortality, and peace we long for, freely as a gift, and so we work—patiently doing good and believing that God's blessing rests on us—because of his work, because he shows no partiality. He always rewards in the same way those who are in his Son: with the blessings he has earned.

Day 7

THE PRAISE OF GOD

For no one is a Jew who is merely one outwardly, nor is circumcision outward and physical. But a Jew is one inwardly, and circumcision is a matter of the heart, by the Spirit, not by the letter. His praise is not from man but from God. —Romans 2:28–29

It's axiomatic to say that people crave approval and praise. We want to look good, to be respected, to be thought well of. We want people to tell us that we're doing a good job, trying our hardest, playing well with others. In some ways, our very normality is tied to our pursuit of self-admiration and of the admiration of others, while depression and self-harm flow out of hopelessness and despair—the belief that obtaining others' good opinion will always be just beyond our reach. It really doesn't matter if we're in elementary school, climbing the corporate ladder, or playing golf in a retirement community; we all long to hear praise.

Stop and think for a moment: how much time, effort, and money have you spent on looking good? I'm not talking here merely about new clothes or diet plans per se but about embellishing your reputation, your résumé, and your outward persona. What would you give to have someone you care about tell you that you're really loved and welcomed after all? The question is not whether you will do this. The question is how you're going to go about it.

Some of us answer the relentless cry for acceptance by saying that we don't care about it. When I was in high school, I wasn't one of the popular kids. How did I respond? I responded simply by saying that I didn't care. I purposely hung out with losers and disdained the cheerleader crowd. I was self-deceived. I assumed that by not trying to be in with the "in" crowd, I was somehow better than they, more authentic, less shallow. Of course, the truth is that I was just as addicted to other people's opinions as they were, just not to the opinions of the same crowd.

Then, when Jesus saved me in my early twenties, I found welcome and acceptance in a new place—the church. This was a revolutionary turn in my life, but, even so, many of the old wants and desires continued to trip me up. I still wanted to be accepted, loved, and welcomed. But rather than pursuing my former identity as a rule breaker, I became a rule keeper and a keeper of the rules for everyone else too. I set about proving that by my rule keeping, I was finally worthy of respect and praise. I also worked to make sure that others were living as they should. This sin resulted in significant conflict with people who weren't doing things the way I thought they should. My thinking went like this: *I have to obey the rules. Why don't they?* I was engaged in a "legalistic battle for supremacy."[6] It also resulted in despair and obsession over whether I was making the grade myself. I admit that the first three decades of my Christianity were not marked by an overabundance of righteousness, peace, or joy. There were days of demands and despair, days of self-indulgence and rebellion, and days of "work for God" that never really seemed to be sufficient. Then, in God's great kindness, he opened my eyes to the power of the gospel to transform me and to free me from the tyrannical rule of man pleasing. He did this by generously lavishing approval on my soul.

Let's look again at Romans 2:28–29. Paul is continuing his argument that not even the most religious person among us is able to stand approved before God. No matter how outwardly good one might appear, it will never be enough to satisfy God's demands for perfection because God's eyes penetrate our tidy outward persona and perceive us as we really are. "For the LORD sees not as man sees: man looks on the outward appearance, but the LORD looks on the heart" (1 Sam. 16:7).

God looks at your heart. He sees not only your outward "churchy" identity; he sees who you really are, why you do what you do, and what you really mean when you proclaim your allegiance to him. This fact should alarm us all. And it would, if not for the gospel.

The good news is that God has done for us what we could never do for ourselves. We cannot circumcise our own hearts. We cannot cut away our love of the world and the world's praise. We cannot obey inwardly, from the heart, loving the Lord and our neighbor perfectly. We will not be able to transform our identity any more than a baby can choose his family name. Paul's point is that God has to do a work in us "by the Spirit, not by the letter." The Spirit has to free us and transform us, giving us a new identity, a new name, a new motive, a new love. And he has to replace our craving for the praise of the world with the praise of God that drowns out all the trivial accolades of mortal man. And the blessed, astounding truth is that this is exactly what he has done!

> For you have died, and your life is hidden with Christ in God. When Christ who is your life appears, then you also will appear with him in glory. (Col. 3:3–4)

> I will write on him the name of my God, and the name of the city of my God . . . and my own new name. (Rev. 3:12)

> And the Lord your God will circumcise your heart and the heart of your offspring, so that you will love the Lord your God with all your heart and with all your soul, that you may live. (Deut. 30:6)

> And I will give them one heart, and a new spirit I will put within them. I will remove the heart of stone from their flesh and give them a heart of flesh, that they may walk in my statutes and keep my rules and obey them. And they shall be my people, and I will be their God. (Ezek. 11:19–20)

Think of it: you no longer have to live for mere human approval. You are freed from trying to approve of yourself. God approves of you because you have a new heart, a new name, a new love, a new desire.

> Believers, having acknowledged their sinfulness and accepted the gift of divine approval, are in a position to reveal themselves as they really are. This ought to make believers the most transparent and childlike people in the world.[7]

He approves of you because you are covered with the righteousness of the beloved Son with whom he is well pleased. You please him. His commendation, welcome, acceptance—yes, even his praise—are yours! Is that enough? Pray that it will be as true for you today as it already is for him.

Day 8

But Now . . . God

But now the righteousness of God has been manifested apart from the law, although the Law and the Prophets bear witness to it— the righteousness of God through faith in Jesus Christ for all who believe. For there is no distinction: for all have sinned and fall short of the glory of God, and are justified by his grace as a gift, through the redemption that is in Christ Jesus, who God put forward as a propitiation by his blood, to be received by faith. This was to show God's righteousness, because in his divine forbearance he had passed over former sins. It was to show his righteousness at the present time, so that he might be just and the justifier of the one who has faith in Jesus. —Romans 3:21–26

In chapter 1 of Romans we learned that the entire pagan world was under God's judgment and wrath for failing to worship the God that creation openly declared. Then in chapter 2 we learned that even the religious community, the Israelites, were under his wrath because although they had been given God's holy law, they failed to obey it, while hypocritically judging others' disobedience. Now, in chapter 3, Paul lumps both the unrighteous and the self-righteous into one group and teaches that "all, both Jews and Greeks, are under sin" (v. 9). He says that "every mouth" that would proclaim ignorance, innocence, or self-righteousness must be stopped and that the "whole world . . . be held accountable to God" (v. 19). For all have "sinned and fall short of the glory of God" (v. 23).

> The harlot, the liar, the murderer, are short of it . . . but so are you. Perhaps they stand at the bottom of a mine, and you on the crest of an Alp; but you are as little able to touch the stars as they.[8]

We are all in the same predicament: guilty, under wrath, and unable to save ourselves. At this point it would be logical for us to despair. After all, if God is the omniscient judge, and if as judge he has determined that we're all guilty, and if he can't pardon us without being unjust (Prov. 17:15), what hope do we have? If he simply lets us walk, what about his reputation, his own righteousness?

Beginning with verse 21 of Romans 3, Paul turns a glorious corner, and there we find three words that have transformed millions of lives, inaugurating an utterly new epoch in human history: "But now . . . God . . ." We were all condemned, lost, hopeless, rightly under judgment, and unable to save ourselves, *but now . . . God.*

> But now the righteousness of God has been manifested apart from the law . . . the righteousness of God through faith in Jesus Christ for all who believe. (vv. 21–22)

Oh, astonishing, transforming, life-imparting, blessed words! What would your life be like but for those dear words? Leon Morris has called verses 21–26 the "single most important paragraph ever written,"[9] while Luther called it "the chief point, and the very central place of the Epistle, and of the whole Bible."[10] Why such extravagant praise? Because these words are declaration of news we've been desperate to hear. It is "good news from a distant land . . . cold water to a parched throat" (Proverbs 25:25 HCSB). Oh, thank God! Oh, praise him that we know something other than the wrath, judgment, and despair we deserve!

The good news is that we've been "justified by his grace as a gift." Justification is a legal term that means that we've not only been declared "not guilty" but also that we've been declared "righteous"! As John Stott puts it, it is his "righteous way of 'righteoussing' the unrighteous."[11] Justification means that our record before God is "just as if we had never sinned." Never sinned? No, never. And while this is wonderful news, it is only half the story. It also means, "just as if we had always obeyed!" We've been given a record of complete righteousness! We've been given the righteousness of God. Our parched souls need a good, long soaking in this enlivening truth today, don't they?

How do we obtain this righteous standing we long for? How is it that we are approved of and accepted? Is it by our obedience, our efforts? No! Paul tells us that this righteousness has been "manifested *apart from the law*." In chapters 1 and 2, he's made that abundantly clear. We can't obey perfectly, and what's more, we won't perfectly obey the law. Then how is this righteousness given? If it's not for the super-disciplined, ultra-holy, how can anyone receive it? It is given as a gift "through faith in Jesus Christ for all who believe." It is a gift, of course. If it is impossible for us to earn it, then it must be given to us completely apart from any work on our part.

But, since it is a gift, is it bestowed upon all? Are all justified? No, this is a gift that is given in response to faith. This righteousness is a gift bestowed upon those who believe that God is generous enough to give it, that he is wise enough to devise a way to do so, and that he is loving enough to suffer in order to grant it to us. But what about our faith, then? Can we claim that our believing earns our justification? No, not at all, because even faith itself is a gift (Eph. 2:8), given by the God who has determined to bless us and make us his. He causes us to believe, and then he blesses us with justification, the gift that this faith he gives deserves. Think of that. He's done it all!

You see, when the Spirit prompted Paul to write, "But now . . . God . . . ," he wasn't pointing Paul down some trivial bypath. No, this "But now . . . God" was everything to Paul. Indeed, it should also be everything to us. In these verses we learn that our faith has to be in Jesus Christ alone, not in ourselves or in another person. We come to believe that we are justified because Christ has redeemed or liberated us from our bondage to both sin and guilt by shedding his blood as the currency necessary to ransom sinners.

Further, we understand that the wrath we richly deserve has been poured out in full upon the submissive Son, who bore it in our place. Finally we have faith that it was God the Father who initiated all this and put his Son forward for us, who now stands justified himself as one who "righteousness-es" the unrighteous and yet remains just himself.

Oh, thank God for those three words, "But now . . . God . . ." Such glorious release and hope are ours! Take them with you today and rejoice in all the work he's done.

Day 9

Upholding the Law

Then what becomes of our boasting? It is excluded. By what kind of law? By a law of works? No, but by a law of faith. For we hold that one is justified by faith apart from works of the law. Or is God the God of Jews only? Is he not the God of Gentiles also? Yes, of Gentiles also, since God is one—who will justify the circumcised by faith and the uncircumcised through faith. Do we then overthrow the law by this faith? By no means! On the contrary, we uphold the law. —Romans 3:27–31

It is the natural bent of every human heart to boast. I do it. You do it. Perhaps you're really clever and don't go around obviously bragging about yourself to others, but you're skilled at eliciting flattery or have learned the sly art of name dropping. Perhaps you only praise yourself quietly in your heart as you compare yourself to others, thinking, "I can't believe they would do something like that!" Unkind thoughts about others always go hand in hand with boasting; judging is just the other side of the coin. In fact, even though it's counterintuitive, even when you're comparing yourself unfavorably to others, you're boasting in your heart. You're saying, "I can't believe that I'm such an idiot. I ought to be better than that!" Here's a little test: how did you respond when I said that you boast? If you said, "No, I don't," you just did. Now, it's one thing to boast to yourself or before others, but it's something else entirely to boast before God and try to impress him.

In this passage, Paul states that our boasting before God as Christians is "excluded" because we're justified by faith in the work of Jesus Christ alone and not by our efforts. What this means is that any words you might use to bolster your confidence before God, even (especially?) in your own heart, are excluded. They are simply not allowed; there is no basis for them. As the old Reformers said, "Justification is by faith alone, in Christ alone."

How often do you avoid God's presence because you haven't been doing well in your walk with the Lord and think he doesn't want to see you? Conversely, how often do you feel that God is happy with you and liable to give you goodies because you've begun your day with prayer and Bible reading and you witnessed to the barista on your way into work? These two scenarios are examples of ways we typically boast: "I'm bad today, but when I get my act together and make up for it, God will accept me," or, "I'm good today, so of course God accepts me." This is how boasting plays out in our daily lives, and Paul says that all of our boasting is "excluded"; in other words, it is not allowed.

Paul tells us that our boasting is excluded by the principle of faith. He writes, "We hold that one is justified by faith apart from the works of the law." This is the reality: while it is the default mode of our hearts to put confidence in ourselves, it is a function of our faith in Christ to say,

> No, proud heart. You cannot boast in yourself. The time for all self-trust has ended, and now all your trust has to be in Christ and his perfections alone.

Only the pride-annihilating message of the cross has the power to destroy our illogical yet intractable faith in ourselves. And only the cross, wet with God's blood, can free us from our despair-generating (yet always illusive) quest for self-approval, liberating us to commend others and ultimately to praise God. If praising others is difficult, if you're always seeing their foibles and weaknesses, that's a signal that you're still trying to approve of yourself and judging others. If your heart isn't ablaze with love for Jesus, if you're wondering if God is, after all, really good, as evidenced by worshipful gratitude and zealous praise, this too is a signal that you're still not free.

But does all this talk about freedom mean that we are completely jettisoning God's law? No, not at all. Paul asks, "Do we then overthrow the law by this faith? By no means! On the contrary, we uphold the law." It's easy to see why Paul would ask this question, isn't it? It's logical to wonder if a life based completely on faith in the law keeping of Another might make us people who think we're free to completely ignore the law of God. Is Paul teaching that our faith makes the law utterly obsolete in the life of the believer? No, Paul says. Rather, we "uphold" the law.

When Paul writes that we "uphold" the law, he's saying that we acknowledge the validity of the law.[12] Is the law valid? Yes, of course. It is valid if, as Paul writes later, "one uses it lawfully" (1 Tim. 1:8). What would using the law "lawfully" look like? For believers, using the law lawfully begins with the understanding that the law can never make us righteous. Paul has already proven that point in chapter 2. So although it is good, it cannot make us righteous, because we are utterly unable to fulfill it.

So, then, if we're unable to obey it, in what way do we still uphold it? Here we come now, back to our discussion about boasting: we uphold the law by saying that although it is "good," we put away all bragging about our personal merit-earning obedience. For believers, obedience to the law has been excised from our religious résumé. The law does not apply in that way any longer because it is "not laid down for the just but for the lawless and disobedient" (1 Tim. 1:9).

So then, what do we do with it? First and foremost, we let its demands make us *grateful for Christ's perfect keeping of it*. By faith we believe that he has kept it perfectly for us, and we boast in him. We brag about how holy and good and righteous *he* is.

Our faith assures us that he earned enough righteousness for every sort of person, for those who are tempted to boast about their law keeping and those who love to brag about their freedom to do whatever they like. United as one faith community we are grateful for Jesus's perfect keeping of the law. We are one family who recognizes that we cannot boast about or trust in ourselves at all, but rather our boast is in Christ alone. Go ahead. Brag a bit today. Show off! Grace-loving Christians uphold the validity of the law in their lives by proclaiming that Jesus has done it all. He has perfectly fulfilled the law. Isn't he magnificent?

Day 10

Expecting a Blessing

For what does the Scripture say? Abraham believed God, and it was counted to him as righteousness. Now to the one who works, his wages are not counted as a gift but as his due. And to the one who does not work but believes in him who justifies the ungodly, his faith is counted as righteousness, just as David also speaks of the blessing of the one to whom God counts righteousness apart from works: "Blessed are those whose lawless deeds are forgiven, and whose sins are covered; blessed is the man against whom the Lord will not count his sin." —Romans 4:3–8

Paul begins chapter 4 by stating that "*if* Abraham was justified by works, he has something to boast about," but haven't we already learned that boasting in our works has been excluded? If Abraham hasn't earned God's approval by his works, how then is it that he is declared or counted righteous? Is he righteous because he was obedient, or is there another source of his perfect standing before God? Yes, oh, glorious truth:

Abraham believed God, and it was counted to him as righteousness. (v. 3)

God's approval and acceptance of Abraham were not due to Abraham's obedience. No, they were given because he *believed* God. You'll notice that this passage doesn't say he "believed *in* God," but rather that he *believed God*. Abraham believed God in the same way that we sometimes say, "Do you believe me?" rather than, "Do you believe in me?" He believed what the Lord had spoken to him.

God had promised to bless Abraham and make him the father of many nations (see Genesis 12 and 15). He had promised him that he and all his children would be blessed above all peoples. And Abraham believed him. He believed that God was both willing and able to do what he had promised and that he wouldn't have promised it unless he was able to do it. And so, because he believed God's promise to bless him, the Lord counted Abraham's belief in God's trustworthiness as true righteousness.

Could obtaining righteousness in God's eyes possibly be that easy? Yes, it can. If you believe that God doesn't lie and that his disposition toward you is one of blessing and goodness, he will bestow upon you all the blessings he's promised. Do you believe him when he says, "I have determined to love and bless you, no matter how you fail"?

You might be thinking, *Okay, I believe that Abraham was blessed because of his faith, but my faith isn't strong like his.* But was Abraham's faith in God perfect? Well, yes and no. Yes, Abraham really did believe. His faith "was a settled conviction that God would do what he had promised, no matter what."[13] It was that sort of faith that justified Abraham.

On the other hand, there were times in Abraham's life when his faith slid terribly, such as when he laughed at God's promise, lied about Sarah's being his wife, and tried in his own strength to fulfill God's promise by impregnating Sarah's slave Hagar. Although the Bible is plain about Abraham's failures, we also read that he "didn't weaken in faith" (Rom. 4:19) and "no distrust made him waver" (v. 20). Now, before we try to reconcile these two seemingly contradictory reports, let's take a brief look at another person who was justified by faith alone: David.

David declares that the person who is truly happy ("blessed") is the one who knows that his lawless deeds are forgiven and his sins are covered. The quote from David that appears in Romans 4:8, "Blessed is the man against whom the Lord will not count his sin," comes from Psalm 32, a psalm in which David was surely remembering his personal failures. Although Psalm 32 may refer to David's obvious sins, it doesn't have to. David was a sinner in all the same ways that we are. Of course, as king he had greater opportunity to abuse his power, but he struggled with the same unbelief, the same knowledge of failure, and the same guilt that we do. But he also knew the veracity of this statement: *Blessed happiness is found in knowing that our sins are covered and that God promises to forgive when we ask.*

Let's go back again now and look at the two differing reports of Abraham. We know he disbelieved, but we also read that his belief was strong and didn't waver. How do we reconcile this? Could it have something to do with his justification? *Even Abraham's unbelief was covered by Christ's righteousness.* When the Holy Spirit reports on *Abraham the righteous*, he sees his faith as being perfect, never wavering. He sees Jesus's unwavering faith as imputed to Abraham. That's how Paul could say later in chapter 4 that Abraham believed that God "gives life to the dead and calls into existence the things that do not exist" (v. 17). God gave life to Abraham and Sarah's functionally dead bodies, and, more wonderfully, he imparted life to their dead, despairing faith. He sustained their faith during every temptation and failure and during the long years of weary waiting for the fulfillment of the promise.

But Abraham isn't the only one that God has blessed like this: God himself also breathes life into the sepulchre where our faith lies moldering under decades of living in a world filled with broken promises, unbelief, and disappointments. He speaks, and our trust is resurrected. He makes us believe that he loves. He creates righteousness where none existed and gives us strength to grasp his goodness. He creates and he resurrects. He sustains and he supplies.

God doesn't demand perfect faith from you or me. He knows that we are frail and that we are still walking by faith without the reassuring sight that we long for. Even when Abraham wavered in his unbelief, the gift of righteousness God had already given in response to yesterday's faith remained completely sufficient. Hear Paul the gospel preacher:

> To the one who works, his wages are not counted as a gift but as his due. And to the one who *does not work* but *believes* in him who justifies the ungodly [the one who cannot, will not, does not work], his faith is counted as righteousness. (vv. 4–5)

If your works are worth something before God, then go ahead and boast. Trust in them and in your great faith. If they amount to anything meritorious, then God's smile upon your life is your due, and your payday depends on you. But if your works are fatally flawed, if your faith is a weak pulse from an ailing heart, then you shouldn't expect anything but wrath from God in regard to your work.

The Lord confirmed his covenant with Abraham by stating in essence, "If I fail to bless you I will take your curse for unbelief and disobedience upon myself."[14] Do you see that's what he has done—not just for Abraham but also for you? On that Friday, Jesus received the wages your unbelief and disobedience earned. When he should have received all the blessing that his sinless life warranted, the Father turned that Friday into a payday for you—but not for him. You get his righteousness applied to your work record; he receives the punishment for your unbelief and wickedness.

In light of all these promises, all his work, all these blessings, why would you want to go back to thinking that you have to work in order to be righteous? Why turn back to thinking that you have to have unwavering faith in order to please him? Will you rest today and simply say, "Lord, I believe. Help my unbelief" (Mark 9:24)? He has determined to bless you and love you. Expect his blessing. Believe, and when you don't, believe again.

Day 11

A BLESSING TO THE WHOLE EARTH

For the promise to Abraham and his offspring that he would be heir of the world did not come through the law but through the righteousness of faith. —Romans 4:13

So far we've spent most of our time considering the subjective benefits that are ours through belief in the gospel: we are loved, forgiven, justified, and adopted. We have the "righteousness of faith." Abraham, too, had a relationship with God based on the Lord's promise of blessing for faith rather than as a payment for work done. Yes, ultimately Abraham did respond obediently to God's promise and call, but the promise of blessing came *before* the injunction to obey was given.

Our gospel inheritance is meant to cause us to rejoice and to live out each day in grateful obedience. But our transformation as individuals is not all that's inherent in God's vow to bless, nor are his promised benefits merely for us alone. His kingdom encompasses the whole world; his grace is too infinite to bestow on only one person or even on just one family group. In fact, he is so generous that millions and millions of people will ultimately receive his grace. He declares that his children will be as numerous as the stars of the sky or the sand on the sea.

In reminding us of Abraham, and the promise that was made to him by God when he called him out of his country, we learn that the promise was not meant as a blessing for Abraham alone but that the Lord intended to use him as a channel to bless the whole world far beyond Ur, his homeland. This worldwide blessing would come through Abraham because he was a forefather of Jesus Christ, the one who would inevitably conquer and receive all the nations as his own and then offer them up as a love gift to his Father (1 Cor. 15:28). Here's the promise that God made to Abraham:

> I will bless those who bless you, and him who dishonors you I will curse, and in you all the families of the earth shall be blessed. (Gen. 12:3)

Despite the terrible fall that occurred in Eden, God had predetermined to bless the whole earth through one fallen man, Abraham. Now, quite obviously that blessing wasn't meant for just one family or one nation, nor would any one fallen man (no matter how great his faith) have the capacity to bring worldwide blessing. The world would have to look for someone other than Abraham. Paul demonstrates this in his epistle to the Galatians by quoting Genesis 13:15 and 17:8:

> Now the promises were made to Abraham and to his offspring. It does not say, "And to offsprings," referring to many, but referring to one, "And to your offspring," who is Christ. (Gal. 3:16)

Jesus, not Abraham, is the offspring who will bestow the blessings of the promises upon the whole world, including both Jew and Gentile. The gospel is the good news that announces the birth of an entirely new race, a race not founded upon any human culture, ruler, region, or epoch. It is a race conceived by grace, gestated in the water of grace, and birthed through the blood of the Savior, who fulfilled all law and bled out for his bride. It may seem strange to say it, but on Calvary he gave birth to his new race because all believers are born into this family through his labor and suffering.

The link to Abraham's blessings is no mere analogy for us; it is reality. There is a direct connection between Abraham and believers, and between Abraham as the one through whom covenant inheritance would come and his progeny Jesus Christ, in whom the promised blessing would be given. Jesus is the absolute father, mother, son, heir, and procurer of our inheritance. "Jesus Christ is the head of the new race. All who are united to him are members of that race, but only because he *is* that race."[15]

I've spent time on this today because I want you to have a clearer picture of what you're part of. Although it may seem to you that your faith is weak or that your little church is barely making it, God's got a different perspective. This perspective was what drove missionaries like William Carey, Hudson Taylor, and Amy Carmichael to spend decades pouring out their lives for the gospel, suffering immense deprivation and persecution even though they saw little or no fruit. This is the perspective that millions of suffering pastors cling to as they labor on in faith tirelessly, only to find at the end of the day that their plans for growth haven't progressed one bit and that their best efforts have resulted in misunderstanding and broken relationships.

It may appear that God's declaration that we will be a blessing to the whole earth will never be fulfilled, that we're just too weak and the difficulties are too great. Personally you might feel isolated, as though it's just "you and Jesus" trying to hang on till the end. I want you to have faith to see that God is doing something bigger and grander than anything you might imagine. I want you to see yourself as part of the plan of the ages, part of God's metanarrative initiated in eternity past and played out for thousands of years in human history, and that will surely be realized in eternity to come. You are part of God's blessing to the whole earth. You are part of a grand family. You are his new race. You can believe without fear of disappointment.

I know that this promise will be fulfilled, and I can be sure that this promised inheritance is ours because I've read the end of the story. John's testimony is true—he's already seen it. Here's what he witnessed:

> And when he had taken the scroll, the four living creatures and the twenty-four elders fell down before the Lamb, each holding a harp, and golden bowls full of incense, which are the prayers of the saints. And they sang a new song, saying,
>
> Worthy are you to take the scroll
>   and to open its seals,
> for you were slain, and by your blood *you ransomed people for God*
>   from *every tribe and language and people and nation*,

and *you have made them a kingdom and priests to our God,*
   and they shall reign on the earth. (Rev. 5:8–10)

After this I looked, and behold, *a great multitude that no one could*
number, from every nation, from all tribes and peoples and lan-
guages, standing before the throne and before the Lamb, clothed in
white robes, with palm branches in their hands, and crying out with
a loud voice, "Salvation belongs to our God who sits on the throne,
and to the Lamb!" (Rev. 7:9–10)

See yourself as you really are today. You are part of God's blessing
to the whole earth. The earth and all its peoples are your inheritance
in Christ.

Day 12

COUNTED AS RIGHTEOUS

That is why [Abraham's] faith was "counted to him as righteousness." But the words "it was counted to him" were not written for his sake alone, but for ours also. It will be counted to us who believe in him who raised from the dead Jesus our Lord, who was delivered up for our trespasses and raised for our justification.
—Romans 4:22–25

God spoke over Abraham, the "father of all who believe" (Rom. 4:11)—both Jew (the circumcised) and Gentile (the uncircumcised)—the most important declaration he ever spoke to man.

Just to refresh your memory, here's the background: at the call of God, Abraham took his wife and household and left his homeland, journeying from Haran to Canaan. He was told that he would be made a great nation and that his name would be greatly renowned. And although Abraham followed God's command, he would have to wait for years and years before he would actually see the fulfillment of this promise. Abraham would have to believe that God was doing something greater than what he could see with his natural eyes. He would have to believe that God was going to fulfill his promise to give him a child through whom the whole earth would be blessed.

After many years and much trouble, Abraham and Sarah remained childless in a hostile land. Then the Lord visited him again in a vision and told him not to be afraid. Abraham had just finished fighting a great battle, even refusing to receive victory spoils from the king of Sodom. Abraham's faith needed refreshing. Perhaps he had begun to fear that after all this time, God had forgotten his promise to bless him with a son and make him a great nation. So the Lord reassured him, "Fear not, Abram. I am your shield; your reward will be very great" (Gen. 15:1). Abraham needed to know that God was going to protect him and provide for him. He didn't need to look to earthly means or try to work things out on his own.

To illustrate the fact that God was going to make a great nation of his descendants, the Lord used the night sky as his flannel graph. He brought Abraham out of his tent and told him to look up. "Look toward heaven, and number the stars, if you are able to number them" (v. 5). In that moment, while Abraham was still childless, when his circumstances hadn't changed one bit, when he was still a homeless wanderer in an alien land, Abraham truly believed that God would fulfill his promise to him. And in that one act of belief, Abraham was given something he could never earn: righteousness. "And he believed the LORD, and he counted it to him as righteousness" (v. 6).

Righteousness is the "fundamental Old Testament virtue characterized by a godly life lived in conformity with the law."[16] In an instant, in one split second, the most desirable character quality was credited to Abraham's account by an act of God's will. He was counted as righteous. Abraham was not counted as righteous because he had done something spectacular or had worked great miracles. In fact, just the opposite was true. All Abraham did was look up and believe that God would fulfill his word.

Now, we know from the record of Abraham's life that although righteousness had been imputed to him, he wasn't sinless from then on. He lost sight of God's promise and listened to Sarah's manipulative counsel, taking her servant Hagar as a surrogate mother for the child God had promised him (Gen. 16:1–4). He failed (a second time) to protect his wife and lied about his relationship with her, saying that she was his sister (Gen. 20:1–2). *Abraham's imputed righteousness did not mean that Abraham was sinless* or that God even expected him to be.

Ultimately, that's the point of *imputed* righteousness. It's not something you can get any other way. It means that when God looked at Abraham, he chose not to see him as sinful. He chose to make him the recipient of all the blessings that a completely righteous man would deserve. Abraham had passed from being a guilty criminal before the bench of a judge to being a welcomed, though terribly flawed, son. The Lord didn't judge him for his weakness, for lying about his wife as a means of self-protection, or for being faithless and using Hagar to try to help God out. No, when God looked at Abraham, he saw him as righteous, as having a life that was in flawless conformity with all of God's will.

It is this promise of an imputed righteousness that transformed Paul, and through Paul, multiplied millions more—we who are all now righteous children of faith. But even before Paul wrote these words, the promise was brought to us in the New Testament through the Lord Jesus himself.

In his evening discourse with Nicodemus, a Pharisee who certainly cared deeply about righteousness and viewed himself as Abraham's offspring, Jesus told him that all his works were ultimately in vain. He told him that he needed to be born again, something Jesus knew Nicodemus was unable to do. And then he gave him the message: "If you want to be righteous and have the blessings of the righteous, you must believe" (see John 3:15–16, 18).

The Lord made this message even more clear in John 6:29, when in answer to the question, "What must we do to be doing the works of God?" he responded, "This is the work of God, that you believe in him whom he has sent." Paul's message of righteousness through faith was not something he mistakenly ripped out of context from Abraham. It was the message of Jesus Christ, who in the Sermon on the Mount made the standard of the law so crushing that any honest person would have to despair and look for another pathway to righteousness. Christ's laws were always given for one reason only: to make us despair of ever doing them and forcing us to transfer our trust from ourselves to God, believing that he is as good as his word.[17]

The glorious declaration, "You are righteous!" was not made only to Abraham and Paul. It has also been made to those of us who believe. What is it that we must believe? Simply this: that God the Father raised God the Son from the dead after punishing him for all our sin. Our faithful husband Jesus Christ was "delivered up for our transgressions and raised for our justification" (Rom. 4:25). Because we are unable to live righteously, because we are sinners not only because we sin but also because we are at heart sinful, unable to be righteous by our own willpower, Jesus Christ had to be delivered up—given over, offered in sacrifice—to the Judge whose wrath is more terrifying than we can ever imagine. Then, in one great act of vindication, in one final exclamation point at the end of the sentence—"You are righteous!"— God the Father raised the Son and declared that we are all justified. "God's approval of Christ at the resurrection results in God's approval also of all who are united to Christ, and in this way results in their 'justification.'"[18]

You no longer need to work to hear the blessed benediction "You are good." If you believe that it is true about you, then today you can live in the glorious liberty of knowing that you don't need to work it up or try to be sinless. Just believe.

Day 13

STANDING IN GRACE

Therefore, since we have been justified by faith, we have peace with God through our Lord Jesus Christ. Through him we have also obtained access by faith into this grace in which we stand and we rejoice in the hope of the glory of God. —Romans 5:1–2

As we move into chapter 5, Paul tells us that one of the benefits of our being justified by faith is that we have peace with God. It's important to notice that the peace we now have because we've been justified by faith is not primarily a subjective feeling, a freedom from worry or anxiety (although it is that), but rather a change in our relationship with the God who rules all rulers.

Living in a democratic republic as I do, it is sometimes difficult to grasp the significance of Paul's declaration. Most Americans would assume that of course God would be at peace with them; after all isn't he the peaceful one who called peacemakers the sons of God (Matt. 5:9)? Many of us today just assume that God would be all about peace. *Of course, we think, he was a little demanding and angry in the Old Testament, but he's sort of turned over a new leaf since then, right?*

For Americans who fought for independence over two centuries ago, it's difficult to imagine life under a ruler we did not elect. The thought of an angry despotic dictator who has unlimited power over us is so foreign as to be unthinkable. Because I want you to understand the shock that Paul's early readers felt, and the joy that Paul himself must have known as he wrote, let me remind you of a few biblical truths, beginning with a story found in the book of Esther.

Esther, a young Jewish girl, had been enslaved in the harem of King Ahasuerus, a man with unrestricted power over the entire kingdom of Persia, which at that time stretched from India to Ethiopia. To say that this man had corrupting absolute power would be an understatement. Having become angry with his former wife, he sought out a replacement and, after months of preparation, Esther was awarded the "prize" of being called his queen.

As the story progresses, Esther soon finds herself in desperate straits. Facing the prospect of the annihilation of both herself and her entire race, she was forced to enter the king's presence, uninvited, to try to influence his decision about her people. Knowing that she was risking her life, she was utterly terrified. She knew there was a good possibility that she would die. Thankfully, we read that when she entered the royal throne room, the king extended to her the "golden scepter" of welcome. It was due to her determination and his reciprocating welcome that she saved many thousands of lives, including her own (Est. 5:1–2).

Although Esther had been a chosen favorite of Ahasuerus, and despite the fact that he had made her his queen, she felt no confidence in entering his presence. She did not know whether he would order her execution or welcome her into his arms. She did not know whether he would be at peace with her or be in the mood to humiliate or annihilate her. Even being his wife didn't guarantee welcome access into the king's presence. What kind of mood was he in? Did he still like her? Would she win favor in his sight? No one could know. She had no grace in which to stand.

The Romans to whom Paul wrote knew all about tyrannical rulers too. Although not the worst in the line of Roman rulers, Claudius, emperor of Rome during the time of Paul's writing, was nevertheless someone to be feared and obeyed. In his quest to restore order to Rome, he forbade the Jews in Rome from assembling and eventually expelled them from the city. Included in this exile were Aquila and Priscilla, believers who had no right to refuse to leave or any legal ground on which to appeal. That any Roman (Jewish or Christian) would have open access to Claudius for appeal or anything other than punishment was completely unthinkable, utterly without possibility.[19]

Paul himself, the one who is telling us that we have been given peace with God, calls him the "Sovereign, the King of kings and Lord of lords, who alone has immortality, who dwells in *unapproachable* light, whom no one has ever seen or can see" (1 Tim. 6:16). Look again: Paul writes that our God lives in unapproachable light: he is inaccessible, we shouldn't be able to cozy up to him.[20] We shouldn't even be able to know whether he's angry or waiting to punish us. At peace with him? Hardly.

Now, let's go back to our opening verses and think about them again.

> Therefore, since we have been justified by faith, we have peace with God through our Lord Jesus Christ. Through him we have also obtained access by faith into this grace in which we stand. (Rom. 5:1–2)

This news of peace with God should simply astound us. The Creator of the universe, who "gives life to all things" (1 Tim. 6:13), who is "the blessed and only Sovereign, the King of kings and Lord of lords, who alone has immortality, who dwells in unapproachable light" is right now, at this very moment, at peace with you (vv. 15–16). You have access by faith into the grace that invites you to stand welcomed and accepted in his presence. This peace gives you confidence that he will embrace you and delight in having your company.

To put it another way, *God is happy to see you.* Unlike Esther, who had to pray, fast, bathe, and put on royal robes in the hope that she would be welcomed by her husband, you've been justified. You're already clean, and you're wearing the most beautiful clothes ever constructed, clothes fashioned out of Christ's righteous works. When you come into his presence, you can stand in confidence and sing:

> I will greatly rejoice in the LORD;
>   my soul shall exult in my God,
> for he has clothed me with the garments of salvation;
>   he has covered me with the robe of righteousness. (Isa. 61:10)

This means that when God looks at you, he welcomes you with the same welcome that he has for his Son because you look like the Son; you're standing in grace.

The grace in which you are standing before the Lord is not "a mere gracious disposition, but an expectation of the Lord's showing kindness."[21] The Lord is no longer at war with you. A cessation of all hostilities has been declared, and in their place he has promised to show you kindness. So enter in. Know that you don't need to get yourself all cleaned up. Jesus has already done all this for you. You have peace with God. Stand in the grace he has given.

Day 14

But How Can That Be Right?

For while we were still weak, at the right time Christ died for the ungodly. For one will scarcely die for a righteous person—though perhaps for a good person one would dare even to die—but God shows his love for us in that while we were still sinners, Christ died for us. —Romans 5:6–8

The message given in the verses above is so shocking that it is, without the Spirit's enabling, absolutely unbelievable. It's not simply that this is hard to believe; it's actually *impossible* to believe if the Holy Spirit doesn't personally put the ability to believe it into your heart. (Maybe you'd better go back and read it again.) If you've found your head nodding in thankful gratitude for Christ's work on your behalf, you've been indwelt with the Holy Spirit and been given the gift of faith.

If you are familiar with this passage, don't let that familiarity blind you to the fact that it attacks everything we've come to expect about how the world works. We have all had it drummed into our heads that *what goes around comes around*. In fact, that's exactly what we teach our children when we tell them that if they're good, good things will automatically happen to them. Our family recently attended a Christian middle-school graduation at which the principal said as much: "Right behavior precedes great opportunities." (Really? Apparently Jesus didn't get that memo.)

Anyway, all of us find great comfort living in and promulgating a quid pro quo world order. We blindly convince ourselves that although we may not be perfect, at least we're trying our best; we're holding up our part of that Latin equation, quid pro quo. Of course, if we were to cease our frenetic rush long enough for some honest self-examination, we'd discover that there really are very few times we try to do our best and absolutely no times when we do so with pure motives. Quid pro quo seems like a good idea only as long as our blinders are securely in place.

Even though inconsistency marks our every thought, and hypocrisy mars even our demand for consistency in others, the truth is that we still believe that we're pretty good, pretty moral, and pretty consistent. We think that life would be better if everyone were more like us: Christians who know what Christianity is all about and live lives that prove it (except in those terrifying moments when the blindfold begins to slip and the truth slams us upside the head).

Contrary to popular belief, Christianity is not a celestial, quid pro quo program where good people become good-er and earn goodies. It is not moralism. It is not a program in which you get your act together so that God will bless you and you can feel good-er about yourself.

I was witnessing to a young woman once who voiced her resistance to becoming a Christian in this way: "I don't think I can be that good," to which I (almost) shouted, "Of course you can't! That's the point!" Every other religion in the world is, in some sense, a moralistic climb up to godhood or nirvana or Allah. In every other form of religion we see a god that blesses those who do his bidding or at least figure out how to appease his capricious whims. In fact, even in my own heart I find a propensity to make this verse say something more along these lines:

> Christ died for us, *on the condition that after a reasonable length of time we would be the kind of people that no one would ever have had to die for in the first place.*[22]

Christians are not climbing up Sunshine Mountain, proving that we don't really need a Savior. Rather, Paul tells us that we are weak sinners, enemies of God (Rom. 5:8) whom he has chosen to die for. We are those upon whom God has showered his love. Far from enabling our climb up Sunshine Mountain, this truth cuts our legs out from under us and lays us in the grave from which God must resurrect us with Christ. The truth is that God has had the last word about who we are and what his remedy is, and that word is one that both slays us and makes us alive. He annihilates all our self-confidence by calling us weak, ungodly enemies, and then in our distress he comforts us by telling us that he loved us so much that he chose to die for us.

When Paul says that we are weak and ungodly, he means that we are *morally incapable of doing good.* We have no moral strength to draw upon to save ourselves. We are ungodly; we belong to a group of people who live "without regard for religious belief or practice."[23] He calls us evildoers. Those words, as hard as they are to believe and really reckon with, are meant to do two things: tell us who we really are and destroy any thought we might have of earning anything from him.

But they're not the only words the Lord wants us to hear. He also says that this is the group of people for whom he killed his beloved Son. Yes, when the perfect time had come, the Father sacrificed him on the altar of his love for us. Sin, death, sorrow, sacrifice, love—welcome.

As you walk through your day today, I pray that your focus would be squarely centered on Christ and his love for you. You'll find it easy to fall back into a quid pro quo mind-set, into thinking that you're fulfilling your responsibilities, so everyone else (including God) should fulfill theirs. Or you'll find it easy to think that your sin is all God sees and that he would somehow love you more if you would just stop being so weak and ungodly and get your spiritual act together. Instead, let me encourage you to believe these unbelievable words: *Christ died for the ungodly.*

Day 15

SAVED BY HIM
FROM HIS WRATH

Since, therefore, we have now been justified by his blood, much more shall we be saved by him from the wrath of God. —Romans 5:9

People these days don't have much of an inclination to believe in a God of wrath. Wrath, especially in a deity, is utterly passé. In fact, I recall one *Star Trek* episode from the late '60s in which I met Apollo, a "god" who was needy, vengeful, immature, and, oh, so lonely.[24] Turned out that Apollo was desperately lonely because all the other gods had given up trying to be gods in light of enlightened mankind's newly embraced unbelief. So they had cast themselves on the winds of the universe, a fitting metaphor for those useless figments of man's benighted imagination.

Apollo alone had held out hope that he could still find some humans who needed him, humans he could love and from whom he would receive the worship he craved. Enter starship *Enterprise* and the crew who held the key to his happiness. Apollo longed for the worship of the *Enterprise's* crew and he wasn't going to take no for an answer. Of course, Captain Kirk wouldn't allow some has-been to derail his mission, so he refused, and Apollo unleashed his terrible wrath. Eventually, like his friends Apollo ended up casting himself on the winds of the universe. So much for *Star Trek* theology and gods of wrath.

I'm sure that the majority of my readers don't get their theology from *Star Trek*, but I wonder how deeply we've been influenced by the belief that a god capable of great wrath belongs more to an ancient religion found in Athens than to one found in twenty-first-century Southern California. After all, we don't need to connect natural disasters to a god of wrath any longer; we've got all the forces of nature figured out. We know that lightning doesn't come from Mount Olympus and that eclipses aren't caused by a cranky god trying to get us to sacrifice a chicken.

In addition, pop psychology has disallowed a god of wrath because the threat of punishment might damage our fragile self-esteem or make us feel badly about ourselves. God forbid! So, instead, even Christians have sought to replace the true God with a god made in our image, a god who is more grandfatherly and benign, an all-accepting therapist type who has nothing but praise for us and certainly never gets angry. After all, he's bigger than that, right? The god of postmodernism might click his tongue over our failures, but he would certainly never punish us in his wrath, would he?

Although we might like this tamer version of god, this isn't God Jehovah of the Bible. No, Jehovah is something else altogether, a God with exceeding wrath for those who refuse to believe that he is as good as he says he is. God's wrath is

> the permanent attitude of the holy and just God when confronted by sin and evil. . . . It is a personal quality, without which God would cease to be fully righteous and his love would degenerate into sentimentality. His wrath . . . is not wayward, fitful or spasmodic, as human anger always is. It is as permanent and as consistent an element in his nature as is his love.[25]

In the same way that God is holy, just, and loving, the Bible tells us that wrath is also a permanent part of his character. It is an element in his nature. Here are a few verses from both the Old and New Testaments to remind you of this truth:

> For the LORD is enraged against all the nations,
>   and furious against all their host;
>   he has devoted them to destruction, has given them over for
>   slaughter. (Isa. 34:2)

> Whoever believes in the Son has eternal life; whoever does not obey the Son shall not see life, but the wrath of God remains on him. (John 3:36)

And you were dead in the trespasses and sins in which you once walked, following the course of this world, following the prince of the power of the air, the spirit that is now at work in the sons of disobedience—among whom we all once lived . . . and were by nature children of wrath, like the rest of mankind. (Eph. 2:1–3)

Then the kings of the earth and the great ones and the generals and the rich and the powerful, and everyone, slave and free, hid themselves in the caves and among the rocks of the mountains, calling to the mountains and rocks, "Fall on us and hide us from the face of him who is seated on the throne, and from the wrath of the Lamb, for the great day of their wrath has come, and who can stand?" (Rev. 6:15–17)

The nations raged, but your wrath came. (Rev. 11:18)[26]

God loves us fiercely. As Mr. Beaver told Lucy in Narnia, "He's not a tame lion," and no matter how much we'd like to re-create him, his character is settled. Because God loves his people fiercely, he is fiercely angry when they refuse him. Although we might not be comfortable with a God capable of such wrath, we instinctively know that deep love *always* engenders deep wrath when spurned. For instance, if I didn't really love my husband, I wouldn't get too worked up if he were unfaithful. *Oh well,* I would think, *what's the big deal?* But if I do love him, if I've invested my life in him, then a natural and proper response would be deep wrath at his infidelity. Think about Aragorn from *Lord of the Rings.* Can you imagine him offering up a bland "Oh well, I guess these things happen" if Sauron had stolen away Arwen? No, Aragorn would unsheathe his sword; Sauron would know his wrath.

The sad and inevitable result of creating a wrathless god is that he will also be a god incapable of deep love. If we don't see how truly angry God can be, we'll never know how truly loving he has been. And we'll always sense that while he may not be really angry, he certainly isn't ever really pleased either. Stripping God of his anger also strips him of his intense love and welcome. If we create a weakly benign, all-accepting god, then we'll never really know love, we'll never be truly forgiven.

Here again is the good news with which we opened this day: "Since, therefore, we have now been justified by his blood, much more shall we be saved by him from the wrath of God" (Rom. 5:9). Because we've already been justified, completely forgiven for everything that would engender his wrath against us by the shedding of Jesus's precious blood, and since we've been given Jesus's perfect record of always obeying perfectly, we've been saved by him from God's wrath.

God has great wrath, but all of it has been poured out upon himself. Unlike some demigod demanding the sacrifice of a chicken or a goat, God took upon himself all the punishment his love required, pouring it upon his dearest. *All* of God's wrath for *all* of our sin has already been spent, poured out upon the Son he loved. Now when God looks at us he cannot see our failures; they are hidden from his view (Isa. 38:17). The record of our adulteries and idolatries and unbelief have been washed away in Calvary's flood, and our Father is now free to pour out all his love upon us without the possibility of wrath. That's because *all* the wrath-engendering sin we ever have or ever will commit has already been hurled into the depths of the sea of his forgetfulness (Isa. 43:25; Jer. 31:34; Mic. 7:19).

It is impossible for God to choose to remember something he has chosen to forget. Yes, he is a God of wrath, but all of that wrath has been removed from you and poured out upon himself. Today you can love him for who he really is and rejoice. You are intensely loved.

Day 16

RECONCILED FRIENDS

For if while we were enemies we were reconciled to God by the death of his Son, much more, now that we are reconciled, shall we be saved by his life. —Romans 5:10

Have you ever had a falling out with a friend? I have. I've felt that inward cringe, the sorrow and dark emptiness that fills my heart when the welcome, free ease, and confidence that had marked our times together are replaced by feelings of shame, anger, or distrust. Perhaps your friend said something or acted in a way that brought division between the two of you. Where once you felt close to her, at ease, able to be transparent and trusting, now there is distance, tension, self-protection, and suspicion. When that kind of destruction happens to a relationship, it's easy to spend hours rehearsing the offense and your response; like a scratched record, the scenario plays over and over in your mind. Perhaps you're the cause of the breakup, so you feel consumed with self-recriminations and guilt. *Why did I say that? How could I? Oh, if only I could go back and make it all right again.* The breakup of a valued relationship feels terrible, doesn't it? I know that it's hard to think about anything else when something like that has happened with someone dear to you.

On the other hand, reconciliation is wonderful. When two friends who have been at odds with one another are willingly brought back into relationship and reconciled, days that felt dark and out of kilter now sparkle with sunshine and peace.

Although reconciliation is wonderful, it's usually very costly. Forgiveness always is. When we choose to give up our right to accuse and to demand repayment for an offense, it will certainly cost dearly because when we've been hurt, we want the one who hurt us to feel our pain. Isn't it our right to demand payment for damages? Forgiving means that we give up our rights and forsake the moral high ground we've claimed as the injured party.

In today's passage, Romans 5:10, Paul again reminds us that reconciliation was purchased for us by the God who gave up his right to demand obedience (and punishment for disobedience) by punishing his Son in our place. When he did this, he reconciled us to himself. He reestablished the relationship we've chosen to destroy. It was far more costly than we can ever imagine for him to do what he did for us.

But that's not all Paul has to say. We've not only been reconciled by Christ's death; we've also been saved by his life. Before we think about what it means to be saved by his life, let's look at the literary device Paul uses to make his point: comparison from the greater to the lesser. Paul's first statement is the greater of the two: we were enemies of God who have been reconciled by Christ's death. The second part of the equation is the lesser of the two: now that we are his friends (now that the most difficult obstacle has been overcome), we will be saved by his life.

Paul uses this same teaching method in another place in Romans:

He who did not spare his own Son but gave him up for us all, how will he not also with him graciously give us all things? (Rom. 8:32)

Do you see the greater/lesser comparison there? If God wouldn't spare his dear Son but gave him up for us, doesn't it stand to reason that he'll graciously give us everything we need? His gracious generosity is on display in both passages: he'll give us everything we need and he'll save us by his life.

His care is a nice promise, but how can we be certain that he'll follow through? We can have strong certainty because of Calvary. He's proven his trustworthiness by doing the hardest thing there was to do: he gave up his own dear Son. If it meant that much to him to be reconciled to you, doesn't it stand to reason that he'll follow through on all his promises to care for you today?

Can you imagine a scenario in which you work for years to save up thousands of dollars to buy a precious diamond ring, only to throw

it in the trash? This analogy is weak and not nearly what it cost your Father to be reconciled to you. He didn't just work for years. He killed his Son and for a brief moment on Calvary deserted him, breaking the relationship with his Beloved so that he could have relationship with you. God was not satisfied with simply allowing us to return to his presence without reconciliation, the way David did with Absalom (2 Sam. 14:1–24). No, God wanted our friendship, so he made a way for us to be reconciled.

Do you realize that you are now, this moment, the friend of God? Do you think about yourself in that way? How does God treat his friends? Would he desert them or leave the work he's doing in them half-done? Do you see that because he has made you, he is utterly committed to your complete salvation? Salvation here includes not only "justification at the start of the Christian life but also completed sanctification, glorification, freedom from final condemnation, and future rewards."[27] Since you've been reconciled, you can be assured that you will be saved, not only on this day but also throughout eternity.

Reconciliation with God is not simply a wonderful theological truth meant to warm your heart when you're in a particularly spiritual mood. No, reconciliation with God impacts all our relationships. It means that we are never alone, never deserted, never friendless.

It is natural in our fallen world to feel alienation from others. None of us ever thinks we truly fit in. Perhaps we walk around in the foyer at church on Sunday morning and wonder why everyone else seems to have someone to talk to. Or, perhaps we do have conversations with others, but we never feel that we're really accepted or loved for who we are. We're always covering ourselves up, hoping that if people begin to know us for who we are they won't desert or betray us.

This alienation began in the garden of Eden when Adam and Eve hid from God and also hid their nakedness from one another. One of the terrible blights of sin is that we no longer feel comfortable with others; we always assume that if we are known, we will be alone, so we cover ourselves up and hence never truly fit in.

The shocking beauty of our reconciliation with God is this: he's the only one before whom we stand utterly exposed, completely known. "And no creature is hidden from his sight, but all are naked and exposed to the eyes of him to whom we must give account" (Heb. 4:13). Think of that. Aside from the Lord, there is no one in your life before whom you are completely exposed. This should terrify us, but there is beauty and welcome here too. Although he knows us completely, he has also determined to be our friend.

We are completely reconciled with him. This truth frees us from our perpetual feelings of alienation, from having to construct fig-leaf false identities in an endless and vain quest to make ourselves presentable while hoping that no one notices what a sham we are. It makes us able to love others because we have been known and loved.

You can rejoice today because, even though you might feel like you're alone, you've got a friend in Jesus, who "sticks closer than a brother" (Prov. 18:24). Run to him today.

Day 17

REIGNING IN LIFE

For if, because of one man's trespass, death reigned through that one man, much more will those who receive the abundance of grace and the free gift of righteousness reign in life through the one man Jesus Christ. —Romans 5:17

This morning while I was preparing to write today's devotional, I received an e-mail from a friend accusing me of sin due to something I had foolishly said publicly at a conference. As I read over my friend's concerns I was able to see and agree with her perspective. I had sinned, and not just in the ways that she was aware of. The Lord enabled me to make a full confession and apology, and, most surprisingly of all, I wasn't devastated by the process. I wasn't beating myself up or filled with chagrin or guilt, nor was I angry, trying to cover up my errors or blaming someone else. I didn't want to accuse this friend in return, either. She was right, and I was astonishingly free to welcome her criticism into my day.

As I've pondered my heart's response to this accusation, I've realized that this freedom I'm experiencing today is only because of the good news of the gospel. Because the gospel tells me that I am more sinful and flawed than I ever dared believe, I'm no longer entrapped in trying to prop up my former flawed identity. I don't have to pretend to be something other than what I am. I don't have a reputation to protect. I can freely admit my failure without needing to cover up, be defensive, or beat myself up. Rather than trying to find a way to protect or justify myself, I am totally free to be who I really am—a very great sinner. Rather than raking myself over the coals, wondering, *How could I be such an idiot and sin like this?* I am now free to say, *Of course I sinned like this! It's just God's grace that I don't get e-mails like this every day! I am, after all, a very great sinner. But that's not all. Not only am I a very great sinner, but I've got a very great Savior.*

The gospel tells me that although there is nothing to recommend me, I've been more welcomed and loved than I could ever hope. What that means is that the Lord continues to love me and welcome me as his dearly beloved daughter, not because of anything that I do but because of the Son's perfections. Elyse, the foolish sinner, has been given an abundance of grace and the free gift of righteousness by the One who sees me as I am in all my sin, hypocrisy, unbelief, and pride and yet continues to call me "justified."

Today I'm deeply aware of his love and welcome. This foolishness of mine did not damage the relationship I have with him; in fact, it has drawn me closer to him, helped me to rely on him, and filled my heart with gratitude for him. It has served to make me more aware of my sin and the wonder of the gospel.

It has also made me thankful for Jesus's perfect keeping of the law in my place. I'm able to rest today in the realization that he spoke publicly thousands of times and never sinned. For me, as a public speaker, *Jesus is my righteousness.* He never boasted; he never talked about how persecuted he was so that others would esteem him more. He never sought glory for himself. He always spoke the truth in love, knew how to say what should be said, closed his mouth when it was inappropriate for him to speak, and opened it boldly in love when the time was right. You never heard his "voice in the streets" (Matt. 12:19). In his words, as well as in his life, he never sinned by failing to love his neighbor. Because of the abundance of grace and the free gift of righteousness, I have that record today. *So do you, if you believe.*

I'll be honest with you. I don't always respond the way I did today. I don't always remember the gospel, that I'm resting securely in his love and life. Sometimes I think I need to protect myself, and I try to claw my way to the top, just like everyone else. But even on those days, on the days I forget what he's done and who he has made me to be, I still have his perfect record. *So do you, if you believe.*

In speaking of our reception of the abundance of grace, Paul uses an unusual Greek word that means not simply "a provision" but rather an "abundant provision," which emphasizes "generosity of God's provision. . . . God's grace is never given with a niggardly hand."[28] His grace is the free grace that we do not deserve.

His bestowal of grace upon us is generosity itself. He doesn't just dole out a little grace here and there. No, he floods our lives with it. Further, in receiving this abundant provision of grace and the free gift of the righteousness of Another, we now "reign in life" (Rom. 5:17).

Throughout chapter 5, Paul has been contrasting Adam with Christ, death with life, and sin with righteousness. Here he tells us that because God has generously flooded our souls with grace and righteousness, we reign in life rather than being reigned over by death and sin. It is not only that Jesus Christ reigns, which is what one would expect to read, but we ourselves are reigning. Of course, Paul is referring in part to the future, when we will reign eternally with Christ (Rev. 22:5), but he's also talking about our ability right now to reign over all of Adam's hateful legacy: both sin and death.

That seems backwards, doesn't it? Doesn't it seem that those who reign in life should be those who have an abundance of determination, who have earned their righteousness through consistent obedience? But Paul says just the opposite. What I've gone through today demonstrates how free grace and imputed righteousness actually make me more, not less, able to confront my sin and grow in godliness. Can you see how I've been able to reign in my life: no longer crushed by the certitude of spiritual death because of my error, no longer enslaved to sin's incessant search for an identity outside of Christ, no longer afraid to admit failure or hopeless that I'll never change, but rather ruling over sin and death right now, in this life, because of the abundant grace of God?

How does all this happen? "Through the one man Jesus Christ," of course. Because God the Son took on flesh and became a human being, because he completely fulfilled all the law in my place, because he died to free me from sin and death, I am able to reign in life today.

It is all his work. Oh, hallelujah! He "breaks the power of cancelled sin, he sets the prisoner free!"[29] And because he's made me drink of this free gift, I've been made to reign today in real life. So, today, don't run from your failure or try to make yourself look better in your own eyes. Instead, refresh yourself with deep draughts of his grace and righteousness.

One Man's Obedience, Part 1

By the one man's obedience the many will be made righteous.
—Romans 5:19

His first conscious thoughts were ones of love. He felt his mother's gentle caress as she wrapped him in cloths meant to keep out the cold. She held him near, and he tasted the sweetness of the milk that sustained him. She spoke words of comfort to him as they fled by night into Egypt. *Shhh, my darling. We must be quiet. We will keep you safe.* She bound him close to her heart, and he rested there securely. He loved her.

He loved being held by his father. He loved his masculine smell and the softness of his beard. He loved feeling the strength in his arms and his voice of command as he spoke to their animals. He even loved his dad when he took him to the temple to be circumcised. He felt pain and shed blood and was accepted into the covenant community, though he did not understand why it had to be like this. He knew nothing but love for his father, though he had caused him to suffer. He loved it when his father sought to comfort him when he cried for hunger or cold or because he needed changing. He did not have words to say so yet, but he knew his father loved him and would one day tell him.

Soon he had a little sister, and with the words he had learned from his parents, he sought to comfort her and tell her of his love for her. She grew to love him in return, but her heart was twisted. She didn't love like he did, so she selfishly kept her toys from him or blamed him for things she had done. Sometimes when he took the punishment she deserved, he sensed that was why he lived. He also had little brothers, four of them: James, Joses, Judas, and Simon, and other sisters, and he loved them all with his whole heart. He was their elder brother. He knew he must protect and love them and always share with them all that was his, no matter how they laughed at him or mistreated him or misunderstood him. He felt how dark their hearts were, and still he loved.

When he was twelve years old the whole family went up to Jerusalem together to celebrate the Passover, as was their custom. He found his way into the temple and listened to the teachers. He sat with them and asked them questions. Everyone was "amazed at his understanding and his answers" (Luke 2:47), and he began to perceive that he loved and understood truth in a way that was different from even those learned rabbis. His ability to comprehend, know, and accept truth had never been bent by sin, and his heart burned as he listened, learned, questioned, and prayed. He loved this beautiful house, his Father's house. He had finally found home.

He sat with the teachers for three days, eating and sleeping only when necessary. His thoughts were being shaped by the best minds in Israel. He heard their discussions about the Messiah for whose advent they longed. He saw the slaughter of the Passover lambs. He heard their cries and smelled their blood. The smoke from their burning flesh stung his eyes, and he knew that somehow his life would bring light and completion and wholeness to all this death. His face was set. He knew now, at least in part, why he lived.

His parents were franticly searching for him, and when they found him they were, like all concerned parents, both relieved and angry. His mother scolded him, "Son, why have you treated us so? Behold, your father and I have been searching for you in great distress" (Luke 2:48). Don't you think their words were accompanied by stinging looks and discipline? His answer was innocent but respectfully incredulous: "Why were you looking for me? Did you not know that I must be in my Father's house?" (v. 49). His parents did not understand what he said to them. They took him away from his Father's house, and again he felt loss. He willingly accompanied them as they went down to Nazareth where he was submissive to them.

Think of that. By this time, he knew where he belonged but he didn't pout or feel sorry for himself or think, *Just when I've finally found my true home, these people take me away! Why don't they understand? I'll show them!* No, he loved them and submitted to them. "And Jesus increased in wisdom and in stature and in favor with God and man" (v. 52).

He had years of growth and mundane obedience yet before him. He was never frantic that he would miss God's plan for his life. He didn't try to manipulate his parents into giving him his way. He was peacefully hidden away. He knew that those years of obedience would be needed by those he loved.

Then his father died; the father that he had known and loved and relied on was gone. He knew he would see him again, but he grieved for the loss and somehow knew this wasn't the first time he had grieved in this way, nor would it be the last. He stepped forward and took upon himself the care of his family, the love of his mother, and the protection of his sisters. He learned the family trade. He worked hard, cut his hands, stood on tired feet, was cheated by customers, and was lied and gossiped about by his friends and neighbors.

He loved parties and telling stories and eating good food and drinking wine with his family and friends, but he never went back for seconds when his hunger had already been satisfied. He never told stories that would embarrass others. He laughed a lot but never at anyone else's expense. He loved women, but he knew that his love was so great that he would never give it to just one of them; he respected them, so he never saw them as chattel to be used for selfish whim. He loved children, and they played on his lap and pulled his beard (gently now), and he listened to their silly jokes and laughed deeply. Men loved and respected him. He was a hard worker, a good provider.

But everyone would say that he never quite fit in. There was something different about him. Everyone agreed he was the most gracious man they had ever met, but still . . .

Then he turned thirty.[30] About eighteen years had passed since he had sat with the rabbis in his Father's house, and now he knew his time had finally come. His cousin John was baptizing in the Jordan River, and he went there to him, to go down into the water of repentance. John recognized him not only as his cousin but also as God's cherished Lamb sent to pay off all the debts of those he loved. John tried to prevent him from such an outrage of humility and obedience, but Jesus said to him, "Let it be so for now, for thus it is fitting for *us* to fulfill all righteousness" (Matt. 3:15).

Even then, Jesus was sharing his righteousness. Jesus was baptized by John, and for the first time in thirty years he finally heard the voice he had longed to hear and had loved to hear through all eternity: "This is my beloved Son, with whom I am well pleased" (Matt. 3:17). At that moment he knew without question who he was and why he'd come. The Spirit, his Spirit, was finally released and flew to him like a dove, granting him the power to live and die and rise again. The Spirit was his without measure.

He did all this for you so that you would have all the righteousness you need today.

Day 19

ONE MAN'S OBEDIENCE, PART 2

By the one man's obedience the many will be made righteous.
—Romans 5:19

Satan had been stalking him for years. Even as a child Jesus had felt that evil, but not the way we feel it. For him, the evil was an alien presence crouching in a corner, watching and waiting in darkness. For us, the evil is within, and when it commands, we answer. Like Jesus, Satan had been waiting, biding his time as he watched the Son's strangely ordinary life. He knew who Jesus was; he had been there at his birth and had tried to slaughter him then, before things got out of hand. But the Father had stopped Satan from touching him. Why? Was it so that he could be a ridiculous, unknown carpenter in a ridiculous part of this little ridiculous planet?

But now, all of a sudden, it appeared that the game was finally on. Jesus was no longer living in obscurity. He had walked out onto the stage of the spiritual cosmos, and Satan's misplaced hopes that Jesus would continue to live in anonymity were crushed. Why was Jesus being baptized? *Blast! Damn! Is that the Father's voice? The Spirit's empowering?*

Rather than hiring a publicist to announce his ministry, the Spirit led Jesus into the wilderness to be tempted by the Devil (Matt. 4:1–11). Jesus walked out into the desert with no food. He prayed, listened to his Father's voice, and learned to rely on the strength of the Word. He became hungry. He was walking onto the field of battle armed with nothing—no great physical strength, no armed soldiers, no fawning entourage or even his angels to protect him. *Everything rested on his obedience.* The war had begun.

The enemy was watching. *Oh, fasting forty days, are you? Goody. I thwarted Moses, the last man who tried this. And, of course, there is the whole fruit-in-the-garden episode and the complaints about manna. No problem. This will be a piece of cake.*

As if he hadn't been there at Jesus's birth, he said, "If you are the Son of God, command these stones to be made bread." *Show off a little. Satisfy your hunger. Let's see what kind of power you've got. Flex a bit, prove who you are.* But Jesus answered, "Man shall not live by bread alone, but by every word that comes from the mouth of God" (v. 4).

Wait—what? You mean the whole food thing isn't going to work with you? Okay then. Come with me to the holy city and let's sit together on a pinnacle of the temple. Now's your time. I understand why you didn't want to make bread. Who wants to waste his power out in the wilderness with no one watching? "If you are the Son of God, throw yourself down, for it is written, 'He will command his angels concerning you,' and 'On their hands they will bear you up, lest you strike your foot against a stone'" (vv. 5–6).

Come on, we both know who you are, let me help you prove it. I'm right with you. Astound these religious insects; demonstrate your power. Wow them. Make your Father do what he's promised to do. You know they're always impressed with these kinds of shows. But Jesus replied, "Again, it is written, 'You shall not put the Lord your God to the test'" (v. 7).

Okay then. I see that you're not going to show off. So let's just you and me go up to a very high mountain, and let me show you what I've got to give. You seem to love this glorified anthill, so let me give it to you. What you see here are all the kingdoms of the world and their glory. Really, what do I want with it? I'll give it all to you if you'll just fall down and worship me. After all, what's the big deal? I can see that you've grown attached to it (though I can't, for the life of me, understand why) and that you want it. So I promise I'll give it to you if you'll just let my ears hear a little teeny-weeny "hallelujah" to me. Such a bargain! Your Father will understand. Come on. Just a little, "Boy, are you great."

But Jesus said, "Be gone, Satan!"

Wait! Stop! Why?

"For it is written, 'You shall worship the Lord your God and him only shall you serve'" (v. 10).

"Then the devil left him, and behold, angels came and were ministering to him" (v. 11). For the first time since his birth, his angels were allowed to intercede directly for the one they loved. They brought him food and drink, and he was grateful.

From that moment on, he preached to the people about his kingdom. "He went about doing good and healing all who were oppressed by the devil, for God was with him" (Acts 10:38). Everything he did every day, every word he spoke, was in honor of the Father he loved and for destroying his enemies' fortresses. He was misunderstood by his followers. His family thought it was time for an intervention and tried to stop him from ministering. The religious leaders, at whose feet he had once sat, hated and envied him. A whore washed his feet with her tears. The masses were hungry, and he fed them. He touched untouchables: lepers, the dead. He shared a drink with a Samaritan slut. He turned over tables and wreaked havoc on religious commercialism performed in the name of piety. He forgave the sins of those looking for physical healing and healed those who had spent decades in darkness and shame.

He spent three years gathering in women and men whom he had loved from before the worlds even began. He called them by name, and when he called them, they left everything and followed. He spent long evenings talking with them; for three and a half years he sought to give them truth. But their hearts were twisted, and though they loved him, they never quite understood what he was saying. Certainly his miracles were wonderful—but his teaching?

There were times when he said things that were so utterly distasteful, so far beyond the pale, such as that whole business about eating his flesh and drinking his blood (John 6:54–56), that they had a hard time holding on. They never understood that he wasn't there to overthrow Rome or elevate them as earthly lords and ladies. Like their enemy before him, they were still hoping he would flex his spiritual muscles and prove to everyone how right they had been to follow him. He knew they didn't understand. He knew they were using him, and he loved them anyway. He knew that he had come to be used.

In all this, he never sinned once. He never disobeyed. He was earning your righteousness. But the most difficult obedience was still to come. He was facing an obedience that would literally strip him of all that he loved and cherished. Everything that made him *him*—all that he knew about himself—was going to be taken from him. For you.

Day 20

One Man's Obedience, Part 3

By the one man's obedience the many will be made righteous.
—Romans 5:19

Pray now and ask for eyes to behold the one man's obedience:

Who do you say that I am? (Matt. 16:15)

You are the Christ, the Son of the living God. (Matt. 16:16)

Jesus began to show his disciples that he must go to Jerusalem and suffer many things . . . and be killed, and on the third day be raised. (Matt. 16:21)

Far be it from you, Lord! This shall never happen to you. (Matt. 16:22)

Get behind me, Satan! You are a hindrance to me. For you are not setting your mind on the things of God, but on the things of man. (Matt. 16:23)

This is my beloved Son, with whom I am well pleased; listen to him. (Matt. 17:5)

Rise, and have no fear. (Matt. 17:7)

The scribes and chief priests sought to lay hands on him at that very hour. . . . So they watched him and sent spies, who pretended to be sincere, that they might catch him in something he said, so as to deliver him up to the authority and jurisdiction of the governor. (Luke 20:19–20)

So also the Son of Man will certainly suffer at their hands. (Matt. 17:12)

The Son of Man is about to be delivered into the hands of men, and they will kill him, and he will be raised on the third day. (Matt. 17:22–23)

And they were greatly distressed. (Matt. 17:23)

Who then can be saved? (Matt. 19:25)

With man this is impossible, but with God all things are possible. (Matt. 19:26)

See, we are going up to Jerusalem. And the Son of Man will be delivered over to the chief priests and scribes, and they will condemn him to death and deliver him over to the Gentiles to be mocked and flogged and crucified, and he will be raised on the third day. (Matt. 20:18–19)

Say that these two sons of mine are to sit, one at your right hand and one at your left, in your kingdom. (Matt. 20:21)

Are you able to drink the cup that I am to drink? (Matt. 20:22)

The Son of Man came not to be served but to serve, and to give his life as a ransom for many. (Matt. 20:28)

What do you want me to do for you? (Matt. 20:32)

And Jesus in pity touched their eyes. (Matt. 20:34)

And Jesus entered the temple and drove out all who sold and bought in the temple, and overturned the tables of the money-changers and the seats of those who sold pigeons. (Matt. 21:12)

And when the chief priests and the scribes saw the wonderful things that he did . . . they were indignant. (Matt. 21:15)

Then the Pharisees went and plotted how to entangle him in his words. (Matt. 22:15)

You shall love the Lord your God with all your heart and with all your soul and with all your mind. This is the great and first com-

mandment. *And a second is like it: You shall love your neighbor as yourself. On these two commandments depend all the Law and Prophets.* (Matt. 22:37–40)

And no one was able to answer him a word, nor from that day did anyone dare to ask him any more questions. (Matt. 22:46)

O Jerusalem, Jerusalem, the city that kills the prophets and stones those who are sent to it! How often would I have gathered your children together as a hen gathers her brood under her wings, and you were not willing! (Matt. 23:37)

You know that after two days the Passover is coming, and the Son of Man will be delivered up to be crucified. (Matt. 26:2)

Then Satan entered into Judas. (Luke 22:3)

I have earnestly desired to eat this Passover with you before I suffer. (Luke 22:15)

This is my body, which is given for you. (Luke 22:19)

This cup that is poured out for you is the new covenant in my blood. (Luke 22:20)

A dispute also rose up among them, as to which of them was to be regarded as the greatest. (Luke 22:24)

Father, if you are willing, remove this cup from me. Nevertheless, not my will, but yours, be done. (Luke 22:42)

And being in an agony he prayed more earnestly; and his sweat became like great drops of blood falling down to the ground. (Luke 22:44)

Why are you still sleeping? (Luke 22:46)

Judas, would you betray the Son of Man with a kiss? (Luke 22:48)

Lord, shall we strike with the sword? (Luke 22:49)

No more of this! (Luke 22:51)

Have you come out as against a robber, with swords and clubs? . . . But this is your hour and the power of darkness. (Luke 22:52–53)

And the Lord turned and looked at Peter. (Luke 22:61)

Now the men who were holding Jesus in custody were mocking him as they beat him. They also blindfolded him and kept asking him, "Prophesy! Who is it that struck you?" And they said many other things against him, blaspheming him. (Luke 22:63–65)

If you are the Christ, tell us. (Luke 22:67)

If I tell you, you will not believe. (Luke 22:67)

I find no guilt in this man. (Luke 23:4)

Look, nothing deserving death has been done by him. (Luke 23:15)

Why, what evil has he done? I have found in him no guilt deserving death. (Luke 23:22)

And when they came to the place that is called The Skull, there they crucified him, and the criminals, one on his right hand and one on his left. (Luke 23:33)

He saved others; let him save himself. (Luke 23:35)

Are you not the Christ? Save yourself and us! (Luke 23:39)

Father, forgive them, for they know not what they do. (Luke 23:34)

This man has done nothing wrong. (Luke 23:41)

"Eli, Eli, lema sabachthani?" that is, *"My God, my God, why have you forsaken me?"* (Matt. 27:46)

It is finished. (John 19:30)

Father, into your hands I commit my spirit! (Luke 23:46)

Now when the centurion saw what had taken place, he praised God, saying, "*Certainly this man was innocent!*" (Luke 23:47)

All that Jesus was, everything he had spent his life building, was gone; those he loved slept and ran away. Everything he cherished was taken from him: his reputation as a good man, his personal righteousness, his purity, his protection and care of his mother; and, most importantly, his relationship with the Father for whose smile he lived every day was gone. He was not vindicated on Golgotha. No, his vindication would come three days later. Instead, he walked sinlessly through death for you: he was ridiculed, tortured, and shamed. Worst of all, he was deserted by his Father.

Think on this: by this one man's perfect obedience, you have been made righteous. Can you see what has taken place? Will you praise the innocent One? Will you rejoice that his innocence is now and forever yours?

Day 21

One Man's Obedience, Part 4

By the one man's obedience the many will be made righteous.
—Romans 5:19

I know I've belabored this point. I hope you understand. I know that by now, you may be hoping that I'll move on. Just humor me for one more day, and I promise I'll be done. I have a goal in mind: I want you to see how obedient Jesus was, and I want you to do so for one reason: so that you'll know what he's given you.

Here's one way to look at how obedient Jesus was, how many decisions to obey he made: He lived approximately thirty-three and one-half years, which translates into 1,057,157,021 seconds. In every second the average healthy human being's brain has "100 billion neurons all firing around 200 times per second," giving a "capacity of *20 million billion firings per second.*"[31] If we want to know how many conscious decisions Jesus made to obey his Father's will, we'll need to multiply twenty million billion by the number of seconds he lived: 1,057,157,021. The equation would look like this: 20,000,000,000,000,000,000 × 1,057,157,021. My calculator doesn't go that high, but I'm sure you get the picture.

Here's my point: *Jesus Christ never made one decision, consciously or unconsciously, in all those innumerable split seconds that wasn't completely consistent with loving his Father and his neighbor.*

Here's another way to think of his righteousness: rather than thinking of it quantitatively (which, I'll admit, is rather overwhelming), let's look at it qualitatively. I might be able (on a really good day) to go through the day without conscious outward sin. I'll admit that really stretches the bounds of credulity to say that, but for argument's sake, let's assume that I'm home alone writing all day and don't have to interact with anyone else and I've had a really good day. Read and prayed in the morning. Didn't overeat. Tidied up the house. No outward sin. But all this doesn't mean that I haven't sinned. It simply means I haven't sinned outwardly. Maybe my motives for staying home and writing are completely selfish: perhaps I'm greedy or ambitious or just like the feel of sitting on my front porch with my Mac. Maybe I love fame. Do you see that although I've spent a significant part of my day looking good outwardly, I'm not even close to sinlessness?

Jesus Christ's obedience wasn't mere outward performance or compliance to external mandates. From the time he had his first conscious thought as an infant, he loved because he loved his Father, and it was his Father's will that he love what his Father loved.

This is what he said about himself: "I always do the things that are pleasing to him" (John 8:29). Sometimes we read statements like that and don't really see what's there. Every second of every minute of every hour of every day of every year of his life Jesus Christ *always* did the things that were pleasing to his Father. Every breath he took was taken in love and worship. Every glance of his eyes, every word he spoke, every action, all had as their goal the glory of God. No matter what it cost him, no matter how misunderstood or misused, he was always focused like a laser on pleasing his Father. He *always* did the right thing, and he always did it for the right reason. Personally, I have to admit that I don't think I ever had even one hour when I could say, "Everything I've done has been solely because I want to be pleasing to the Father."

How much obedience would it take to make millions of people righteous? How much righteousness must one person have in order to overcome every one of our failures and make us completely righteous? Here's the shocking truth: in just thirty-three and one-half years, Jesus Christ was so completely righteous, so perfectly fulfilled the law, and was so flawlessly obedient that when his record is applied to us, we are as Adam was in Eden. Before the fall, Adam was unashamed because he had nothing to hide; he was naked and yet unashamed. But now we're in a better place than even Adam was then: we're not only inno-cent; we're righteous. Isaiah spoke of this great blessing in this way:

I will greatly rejoice in the Lord;
    my soul shall exult in my God,
for he has clothed me with the garments of salvation;
    he has covered me with the robe of righteousness. (Isa. 61:10)

During his lifetime of constant, unwavering obedience, from infancy all the way to death, he wove a robe of righteousness sufficient enough to cover millions and millions of us. Yes, even you.

Through the one act of disobedience of the one man Adam, sin spread death to us all (Rom. 5:12), and we were stripped bare of our righteousness. One representative act of disobedience, one self-plea-sure, one "I think I'll do this my way," plunged us all into sin, ruin, and misery. Ever since then, we've been devising foolish ways to try to cover ourselves up and make ourselves presentable again.

But in Romans 5:19 we hear the good news we've needed to hear since Eden: "By the one man's obedience the many will be made right-eous." Think of that. Jesus's lifetime of obedience has completely reversed the effect of Adam's treachery and made us righteous once again. We look good to God again. We don't have to hide or try to outfit ourselves with new clothes. The only question is whether you will believe.

Now, finally and at last, here's the point we've been working toward all these days. All this righteousness, all Christ's obedience from birth to death, every second of every day—all that perfect suf-fering, all that righteousness—

It's yours right now!

When your Father looks at you, everything we've pondered in the last three days and oh, so much more is yours *right now!* You are righ-teous. Breathe it in. Drink it. Hug it and hold it close. Be crazy happy.

Will you believe?

Be done now with all your stupid efforts to approve of yourself and to look good. Throw them from you! Be revolted by your own goodness and your love of reputation! Shed that old identity the way a snake sheds a skin that's become too constricting and worn. Lose that tired wineskin and pour the delicious, sweet, intoxicating wine of Christ's imputed righteousness into your new life. Don't worry—that new wineskin won't burst. Dance a lot. Brag a ton about how righteous he's made you. Show off your new clothes! Be as free as a drunk to look stupid and hop about for joy. Weep over your sin. Rejoice over his obedience.

All those lessons about how to keep your religion dignified and presentable will be completely blasted away in the raucous party that will be known as "heaven." Oh, my brothers and my sisters! Be free! Taste what is yours right now. Because of the one man's obedience, you are righteous—period. There is nothing more to be said.

Day 22

OF DEATH AND LIFE
AND THE POWER OF
A NEW IDENTITY

What shall we say then? Are we to continue in sin that grace may
abound? By no means! How can we who died to sin still live in it?
—Romans 6:1–2

Romans 6 marks a transition from Paul's primary focus on justification to sanctification, which is that unspectacular, steady change into
Christlikeness that marks the life of the believer. But don't be con-
fused. While it is true that Paul is making a transition here, we mustn't
assume that now it's finally time to put the focus squarely on ourselves. No, the focus will remain exactly where it belongs: on Christ
and what he's done on our behalf.

> Sanctification no less than justification springs from the efficacy of
> Christ's death and the virtue of his resurrection. If the mediation
> of Christ is always in the forefront in justification it is likewise in
> sanctification.[32]

In both our justification and our sanctification, Jesus Christ must
remain in our minds where he is in Paul's: completely, utterly, permanently, gloriously preeminent.

In our passage today, Romans 6:1–2, the apostle presupposes all-
too-common concerns about "too much" grace and poses the question the morality police have been asking for two millennia: "Won't
all this talk about grace encourage the slothful to sin in the name of
graciousness? Seems like you're saying that we should sin so that grace
may abound."

While it is true that some antinomian (one who is "against" the law and believes that Christians can ignore it) somewhere might look at Paul's description of God's super-abounding grace in response to our super-abounding sin and say something innately absurd like, "Well, if all our sin serves to glorify God's great grace, then let's get on it and sin more and more, so he'll be glorified more and more," Paul doesn't respond to this absurdity by downplaying God's free grace and the imputation of righteousness to *all* who believe. He doesn't tell us that now it's finally time to get out our list of imperatives (commands), because Paul knows that a new list of rules won't transform the antinomian's heart. Rules won't make sin lovers obey, because the real problem is not outward behavior but inward loves. No, Paul doesn't use this opportunity to finally give us the law we expect to hear in response to the claims of "too much grace." He goes in an entirely unexpected direction. He tells us about death and resurrection and more about our union with Christ through the work Jesus has already done for us.

Paul's answer is simply this: "How can we who died to sin still live in it?" Notice that he roots our transformation in death and life and that he uses the words "died" and "live" in contrast to one another. *How can we who are dead to something (sin) live to it at the same time?*

This is Paul's primary answer to those who are concerned about talking too much about grace; our new identity is that we've literally died to sin. This death is a once-for-all definitive act that occurred in the past. The believer no longer lives under the domain of sin; he has been "translated to another realm."[33] This happened through our union with Christ in his death, burial, and resurrection as is demonstrated at our baptism. Paul doesn't give us new, more stringent rules to live by. No, he tells us *who we are. It is the realization of our new identity that will ultimately and at heart level transform us.*

He continues on to say:

> Do you not know that all of us who have been baptized into Christ Jesus were baptized into his death? We were buried therefore with him by baptism into death, in order that, just as Christ was raised from the dead by the glory of the Father, we too might walk in newness of life. For if we have been united with him in a death like

his, we shall certainly be united with him in a resurrection like his. (Rom. 6:3–5)

Paul's invoking of baptism rather than commandments as the reply to the phantom antinomian's question speaks volumes. He knows what rules do; he's suffered under them his whole life, and he knows that rules are powerless to transform. Only new life from an outside source will ever change us.

Paul's point here is clear: cavalier ungodliness is utterly absurd given the reality of the death our baptism represents. Yes, once we were enslaved to sin, but that old sin-enslaved person is gone. Our death, signified in baptism and made all the more sure by our burial in the water, is in union with Jesus's actual physical death that was made all the more certain by his burial in the tomb. Here's what Paul is saying in essence:

> Don't be such an idiot! God's gift of imputed righteousness won't make you love sin more for one simple reason: your old sin-loving life is over and gone. It's dead and buried—under the water! Realize who you are! When by faith you accepted that gift of righteousness, it brought with it death and new life.

Baptism means that we'll no longer search out lame excuses to sin, because we've been united with Christ in his resurrection. We've got a new life; we were raised with Jesus by the glory of God the Father.

It seems to me that this concept of our death, burial, and resurrection is a difficult one to wrap our brain around, since it appears for all intents and purposes that we're still alive and kicking. So here's an analogy that might help. The present life of my husband, Phil, is made up of thoughts, desires, emotions, and actions that identify Phil as Phil. The patterns of his thoughts, desires, and deeds would make him recognizable to me, his wife, even if his outward appearance were somehow changed. So when Phil dies, if I'm still alive, although his body will be gone, my memory of him will continue to live on.

In the same way, when we are united by baptism into the death, burial, and resurrection and new life of Jesus Christ, the memory of who we once were remains even though that old person is really and truly gone. The shell of what Phil once was—the reality of his former desires, affections, habits, and inclinations—will have died, but my memory of them will certainly continue to live. In the same way, although we are completely new in Christ, having died, been buried, and been raised to new life, the lingering imprint of our old habits, desires, fears, and unbeliefs still lives on in our memory.[34]

Don't you see that it is the message of God's slaying and resurrecting grace *alone* that transforms us and emancipates us from our old identities with their enslaving loves and desires? Bare rules won't change our memory of who we were; in fact, rules alone will harden us in unbelief because we will always fail in some way to obey them. *Then our failure will remind us of our old identity and lie to us: it will tell us that we're really not changed after all. We're not new; we're just the same as we've always been.* It takes faith to believe that we've really changed, and only the gospel engenders faith.

Our minds need renewing in the light of the transforming mercies of God (Rom. 12:1–2). We need to soak ourselves in what he says about us: we are altogether completely new, as Romans 6:7 says in a more literal translation: "He who has died has been *justified* from his sin."[35] The old you and all the failure, sin, selfishness, and unbelief that was you and perpetuated sin in your old life is under the water, without air, dead, and buried. Your baptism stands as the door that has been forever closed on your old life. You have been given a completely perfect record, raised to new life by the glory of the Father, and that new life isn't a wishful fallacy. It's the truth.

Day 23

REMEMBER WHO YOU ARE

So you also must consider yourselves dead to sin and alive to God in Christ Jesus. —Romans 6:11

Here we are, finally at the first command, or imperative, in the book of Romans. Paul's point in waiting this long to tell us about our responsibilities is that this story isn't about our deeds but about deeds that have been done on our behalf by Another.

Without belaboring this point, I wonder if a person who knew nothing about Christianity aside from sermon and book titles would be shocked by Paul's tardiness in getting around to the steps we need to take. Contrary to popular belief, the gospel is not about finding a life coach who will help us get our act together, nor is it about psychological understanding or morality or political action groups or growing your own wheat. The gospel is the news about Jesus's incarnation, sinless life, substitutionary death, bodily resurrection, ascension, and reign—period. Because it is about him, the emphasis in Paul's great treatise on the gospel will always and unswervingly be Jesus.

But, again, here we are at the first command that Paul gives his readers. Interestingly, it is not a command to hop up off our couches and get to work; it's a command to think, to remember, to realize. It is a command to remember and then to believe what we've remembered as we face our day. What do we need to remember? We need to remember how what Christ has already done transforms who we are right now—not later, once we get it together, but right now in all the messes we've made.

> If Christ's death was a death to sin (which it was), and if his resurrection was a resurrection to God (which it was), and if by faith-baptism we have been united to Christ in his death and resurrection (which we have been), then we ourselves have died to sin and risen to God.[36]

The first command is simply this: *remember.* You are dead to sin because Christ died to sin. You have been raised to God because Christ was raised to God. In your baptism you were united with him in *all* that he has done, and you are now free to serve him out of deep gratitude.[37]

Where sin is concerned, you are to count yourselves among the dead. Interestingly, this first imperative is a command to do nothing except believe what's already been said about you. You are to believe that you are, in fact, dead to sin.

This process of remembering is so crucial to our spiritual life that Jesus himself instituted two sacraments that are to be regularly practiced in our churches: baptism and Communion. Both of these signs are given to us as visible, physically experienced reminders of the good news. Not only does Paul tell us to remember our baptism and its significance, but in 1 Corinthians 11:24–25 he also directly quotes the Lord Jesus, who commands us while partaking of Communion, "Do this in remembrance of me." The Lord Jesus is well acquainted with our propensity to forget unless we actually have something we can regularly see, taste, feel, smell, and touch. He knew that he had to give us something tangible, something that our poor unbelieving hearts could grasp onto.

So he gives us water, bread, and wine, elements available in every culture—normal, ordinary components of daily life. In seeing and remembering the water we think again of our death, burial, and new life. We remember his death, his burial in the tomb, his resurrection by the glory of the Father. In eating the bread we remember the body broken for us: Jesus, the sinless man who walked perfectly through every temptation we face, was crushed for us. We remember a body beaten. He experienced true human death. In drinking the wine we remember the blood that poured from his head, his hands, his feet, and his side, and in that cleansing flood, priceless beyond measure, we know that what we once were has been borne away by his "life-giving flow."[38]

Oh, hallelujah! Are you seeing? Do you remember? In that remembering, real grace is communicated to us through those simple means; a real strengthening and enlightening grace is diffused into hearts that are truly new, yes, but still remain all too human.

The Holy Spirit's initial and primary method of helping us fight sin and live as servants of God does not start with a command to live right (although Paul does get there). It starts with a command to remember and to see ourselves as we now are: truly dead, yet alive in union with Christ. It is this truth—and nothing else—that will engender the desire and motive for grateful obedience in us.

> Once we grasp this, that our old life has ended, with the score settled, the debt paid and the law satisfied, we shall want to have nothing more to do with it.[39]

So, even though sin still seems so alive in me, I must daily and by faith, consider myself dead to it and alive to God. I need to consider everything that God has said to be true about me right now. And when that old sin slave within my heart wants to forget and fall back into old patterns, I need to remind her (and forcefully at times), "Shut up! You're dead." Sure, her memory lives on, but her power to enslave and bend me to her will is now gone. She's a phantom. I have new life. I know this because Christ has risen from the dead.

How can I consider myself dead to sin? I have to believe that when God says I died, I did; that when he said I rose again, I did. It happened in this way: Christ gathered me to himself when I was yet unborn. He took me with him up Calvary's hill, and with him there on that cruel cross a transaction occurred. No, I wasn't there physically, but I was there truly. My old self, the life I once lived, trying to make myself righteous through my own works, was over before it really began. And then, after three days in the tomb, I was resurrected with him. He has gathered my life into his and made me one with him. When I am tempted to sin now, I can say,

> I no longer need to do that. That old Elyse who thought she needed to claw and cry and demand and manipulate is gone. Not just psychologically gone, but really and truly dead and out of the picture. I have been "brought from death to life" and I am now an instrument for righteousness. Oh, Lord, help me remember and believe the truth today.

Day 24

UNDER LAW, UNDER GRACE

For sin will have no dominion over you, since you are not under law but under grace. —Romans 6:14

The opening question of Romans 6, "How can we who died to sin still live in it?" (v. 2), is answered by Paul in a surprising way here at the end of the opening section of the chapter. In the preceding verses, he's given us some pretty clear imperatives:

> Let not sin reign in your mortal body. (v. 12)

> Do not present your members to sin as instruments for unrighteousness. (v. 13)

> Present yourselves to God and your members to God as instruments of righteousness. (v. 13)

At last! you might be thinking. *Finally, a list of commands!* While it is true that Paul is giving us imperatives in verses 12–13, in verse 14 Paul does an astonishing thing. He doesn't negate the commands, but neither does he tell us that now it's "bootstrap" time. No, he jumps right back into the gospel indicatives (declarations) again and makes a glorious promise: "Sin will have no dominion over you." This statement is not a command—"Don't let sin have dominion over you"— but rather a guarantee: "Sin shall certainly not be your Lord—now or ever!"[40] If we think deeply about the commands he's just given, this promise is exactly what we need to hear.

Doesn't it seem like Christians are always looking for the secret to freedom from their bondage to sin and failure? So Paul follows this glorious promise of victory with an explanation that pastor and theologian John Stott called the "ultimate secret of freedom from sin."[41] Oh, and what a secret! Here, right in broad daylight, this secret is revealed for all to see. Sin will have no dominion over you for one simple reason: *"you are not under law but under grace."* There it is, right there—the secret to living a life unencumbered by sin's dominion. Sin's domineering power in our life is obliterated because we are no longer under the law—we are under grace!

When Paul uses the word "under" (as in "under" law or grace), he is referring to being under the control of or under obligation to something or someone, to being governed by something or someone who has power over you. Christians have been released from the tyranny of the law's sin-engendering demands. They are no longer under the law's "power, rule, sovereignty [or] command."[42]

This truth about our release from the law and victory over sin turns everything we assume about how to grow in holiness on its head, doesn't it? *Living under the law, piling on more and more rules, will make you sin more, not less. Always and in every case, and without fail, the law engenders more and more sin.* The person who is under law, "upon whom only law has been brought to bear, whose life is being determined by the resources of law, is the bondservant of sin."[43]

Shockingly, believing that we have to perform in order to avoid condemnation and earn favor does not make us obey; in fact, it does the opposite. It occasions sin. Sin will have dominion over you when you are under law, when you consider yourself still alive and responsible to the law's demands. The law does not lessen sin's grip on your life. In fact, it makes it tighter.

Paul can make this astonishing promise of freedom from sin's domination because he remembers and believes what God has proclaimed. We are no longer under God's condemning gaze; his eye is not the eye of Sauron, looking for men (or hobbits) to destroy. No, now his smiling countenance rests upon us, and all the blessings of grace, favor, and merit are ours today. Because we are now under grace, it is not possible to lose any of the blessings that grace confers upon us, because we were transferred out from under the law's jurisdiction. We are not under law. The law's authority to condemn and cut us off from God's favor is no longer in force.

Here's an example that might help. In the little retirement community where we live, there is a rule that no one can park a car on the street at night. So, if we have guests who stay late, they have to move their cars to one of the lots, or the neighbors will surely complain, and the community manager will be paying me a visit to show her disapproval. If I keep it up, I can even be fined or, I suppose, ultimately expelled. Right now, I am living under the law of this community. Now, if Phil and I were to move to a different neighborhood, the law about parking would no longer apply and the favor of the neighborhood could not be forfeited for our nighttime street parking.

Do you see? You are no longer under the dominion or tyranny of the law. It's no longer possible for you to get a nasty visit from God, because everything that would have occasioned such displeasure with you has been done away with! *You are not under the law; therefore, you cannot break it.*

> It is in the assurance of the continuance of this new status that the believer can go forth boldly and confidently to wage war against sin.[44]

Today we are free to present ourselves to God as his children, and we don't have to worry that he'll write us up for failure to serve perfectly, or even at all. We don't have to come to him and present our record to him as a way to earn favor; we don't have to worry in any way about what the law says about us, because the law no longer applies to us.

The key to being free from the dominion of sin is that the sin-provoking, heart-condemning, faith-slaying law no longer applies. *Park where you want, when you want.* It won't change God's disposition toward you one whit, because there are no parking rules in his kingdom. Does that freedom scare you? The Lord is the neighborhood manager, and he has decided to bless you with all his favor and love, no matter where you park. Jesus parked perfectly in your stead, and the Father has chosen to treat you as though you were the one who had done so. He has released you from any obligation to park properly in the future. The law about where to park has been forever silenced. No law, just grace now and forever.

My guess is that you're feeling a little nervous right now and that you're tempted to ask the same question that Paul does in the next verse: "Yes, but, but . . . are we to sin because we are not under law but under grace?" to which I respond, "You can if you want to. But *God forbid* that you would want to in light of all he has done. Why would you want to put yourself back in any kind of slavery?" You've been freed from the law! You've been given unmerited favor, blessing, and love. Does that kind of love make you want to sin? Does that kind of freedom make you miss being a slave?

God frees us from sin's dominion by changing our desires, not by reiterating the law's requirements. He gives us a taste of the freedom that's now ours: freedom from the law, freedom from sin. When the law says, "Don't park there," it makes you want to, doesn't it? When, on the other hand, grace says, "Park where you want because I've already punished my Son and completely freed you from any parking obligations," this love makes you love your neighbor and not park anywhere that might inconvenience him. It makes you love freedom and resist slavery either to the law or to selfishness.

Now, what do you want to do? Do you feel your heart being warmed with concern for your neighbor? I do. That is why sin won't dominate our lives. Sin can't dominate a life that's been given that kind of freedom, that depth of grace. Drink deeply of his gracious favor to you and then, remembering his grace, park where you want.

Day 25

God Forbid!

But thanks be to God, that you who were once slaves of sin have become obedient from the heart to the standard of teaching to which you were committed, and having been set free from sin, have become slaves of righteousness. —Romans 6:17–18

Right about now you may be wondering if I'm telling you that it's fine to go ahead and sin in any way you want. If the law no longer has jurisdiction over us, does that mean we can live any way we want? I'll answer that question with a weak and qualified yes and a very strong "God forbid!"

In one sense, the law has been abrogated as a way to earn favor with God as regards your standing with God. But the moral law is still in effect as an appropriate response in gratitude for the grace you have already been given. You are under grace, so park in the street if you must, but do so remembering what your sin has cost him.

On the other hand, and this is where we'll spend some time thinking today, the answer is a resounding no, or as Paul emphatically replies to his question, "Are we to sin because we are not under law but under grace? By no means!" (Rom. 6:15).

No, it's not okay to live a debauched life or break restrictive community rules willy-nilly. Why, if the law has been outlawed, is it still not okay to sin with impunity whenever we want? Even though we are free from the law's demands as a way to earn God's smile, there are three other reasons to seek to live a holy life. The first has to do with freedom and slavery, the second with your heart's motivation, and the third with ultimate consequences. So, even though you are freed from the law's demand that you obey in order to earn God's grace, there are significant reasons to resist sin's enticements. Let's talk about them now.

The first reason is simply this: you've been set free from the crushing burden of the law, so why would you now want to become enslaved to the crushing burden of sin? If you continue to give yourself over to sin, you will become a slave to sin (v. 16). Sin exerts a powerfully enticing influence on us. Sin itself is addicting, as Jesus warned in John 8:34: "Everyone who practices sin is a slave to sin." It also hardens our hearts and lies to us, as Hebrews 3:13 demonstrates: "Exhort one another every day . . . that none of you may be hardened by the deceitfulness of sin." It is both enslaving and deceptive, as Edmund learned when he ate Turkish Delight in Narnia, or as Gollum, Bilbo, and Frodo learned when they tried to carry the Ring of Power near their hearts. The longer you dally with it, the more enslaved by it you will become. Don't be fooled:

> Can a man carry fire next to his chest
> and his clothes not be burned?
> Or can one walk on hot coals
> and his feet not be scorched? (Prov. 6:27–28)

You can't play with it or present yourself to it and expect that it will not ensnare you. James 1 is chillingly clear on this point:

> Each person is tempted when he is lured and enticed by his own desire. Then desire when it has conceived gives birth to sin, and sin when it is fully grown brings forth death. (James 1:14–15)

In this passage James employs a "fishing metaphor for drawing prey away from shelter in order to trap them with a deadly hook."[45] Picture this: you're a little trout, safely swimming around under the dock, when you spy what looks like a yummy worm wiggling around on the top of the water. You wonder about it. There does seem to be something a little unusual about it, but you're hungry, so you swim toward it and swallow it down. You know the rest of this story, don't you? Don't be fooled. *You no longer have to obey as a means to earn God's favor, but, on the other hand, you don't want to be flopping around on the dock.*

The second reason that Paul cries out, "God forbid!" is closely linked to James's warning: It is desire that makes you want to sin. Look again at what he says: "Each person is tempted when he is lured and enticed by his own desire." That word "desire" there is so significant. It is a word that is commonly translated "lust," and it denotes something we long for very much. Our primary problem with sin flows out of our desires, the things we long for intensely. These desires function like idols in our lives: they are what we serve, obey, and are willing to sin in response to.

Remember now that the Lord's antidote for our twisted desire is not more law, as we've been saying, but rather astonishing grace. God changes us at the deepest levels of our heart, in our motivating desires, by flooding us with his love: "We love because he first loved us" (1 John 4:19). This is the key to changed desire and victory over sin's allurements. When that little worm is wiggling up on the surface of the water, those of us who have been drenched in his grace can now respond, "Yes, little worm, at one time I might have thought you would be delicious, but the truth is that I've got something so much more satisfying that you actually don't have any power over me now at all. Flop away, little worm; my belly is already full of delicious bread and wine."

Can you see why Paul practically screams, "God forbid!" when he poses the question about our continuing in sin? It is absolutely unthinkable that our hearts would want to eat a soggy worm when we've just had such a satisfying feast. We've been loved, and everything we ever thought we'd need (and more) has been graciously given to us in the Son who loved us and gave himself for us.

The third reason we don't present ourselves to sin is that it will eventuate in death. James's metaphor of the gullible fish ends with these words: "Then desire when it has conceived gives birth to sin, and sin when it is fully grown brings forth death" (James 1:15). In Romans 6 Paul writes, "But what fruit were you getting at that time from the things of which you are now ashamed? For the end of those things is death" (v. 21), and, "The wages of sin is death" (v. 23). Continually giving ourselves to sin will eventually lead to death. Be careful here to understand that Paul is "not implying that believers can actually lose their salvation but that sinning leads them in that direction, away from full enjoyment of life with Christ."[46]

Because our hearts are naturally bent toward the law, continual sin will strip us of faith in all that the gospel says about us. We will find it increasingly difficult to believe that we've been set free from sin, from the law's power to condemn, and that God's smile is resting upon us if we continually give ourselves over to what we know we should avoid. Sin strips our faith, and it leads to ultimate deadness in our lives.

We have been set free from the law's demands and already live under the gracious smiling countenance of a loving Father, while we await our reunion with our Beloved Husband. In light of these truths, today we're to wage war against all our unbelief: our desires that lie to us and tell us God hasn't given us everything we need, our failure to remember that we're free from the law as a way to earn God's favor, and our incredulity at God's overwhelming love for us. You're free to park wherever you like. But why would you park in the street, now that he's built such a beautiful and safe place for you?

Day 26

FREED TO SERVE THROUGH DEATH

Or do you not know, brothers—for I am speaking to those who know the law—that the law is binding on a person only as long as he lives? . . . But now we are released from the law, having died to that which held us captive, so that we serve in the new way of the Spirit and not in the old way of the written code. —Romans 7:1, 6

I'm old enough to remember when the United States employed a mandatory military draft or conscription. I was in high school during the height of the Vietnam War, and all my male friends had to face the very real probability of spending time in military service, whether they wanted to or not. Some young men were given deferments if they were in college, but most of my friends ended up in battles on the Ho Chi Minh Trail and in the Tet Offensive. They were forced to fight or else flee to Canada as conscientious objectors. Even today, the Selective Service System remains in place, and all United States males between the ages of eighteen and twenty-five are obligated to register, even though the draft was discontinued in 1973. There is, of course, one other way of avoiding the Selective Service: you don't have to register for the draft if you're dead. The dead are not obligated to obey the draft law.

Paul opens his discussion about the power of the law to enslave and crush us with a surprising statement. He does not say, "Sure, obeying the law is hard, but if you really work at it, you'll make great progress." No, instead he says, "Do you not know . . . that the law is binding on a person only as long as he lives?" (Rom. 7:1). He says that we who believe, who have already been justified, have been freed from the law's power to bend us to obey it, and we are free for one simple reason: we are dead! In the same way that a misdirected letter from the Selective Service would be returned unopened with "Recipient

Deceased" on the envelope, the law's ability to subjugate us should be returned by our consciences, "Recipient Gloriously Deceased."

We have died with Christ and have been raised with him, and the law has been fulfilled or completed perfectly through our union with him. The law's exasperating and relentless claim has no right to speak to us any longer because Jesus Christ has silenced it forever. When our consciences accuse us, we can sing, "Recipient Gloriously Deceased!"

The reason that we have to see ourselves as dead to the law is that although it makes demands on us, it doesn't give us the ability to obey it. In fact, what it does is engender disobedience. Paul writes that we are not helped on our way to righteousness by the law but that our sinful passions are aroused by it. He writes, "I was once alive apart from the law, but when the commandment came, sin came alive and I died. The very commandment that promised life proved to be death to me" (vv. 9–10). *More and more rules won't make us righteous. In fact, what they will do is engender and arouse more and more sin.*

Knowing from his personal experience the impact of the law on the heart of a sinner, Paul boldly declares the only news that has the power to transform us: "But now we are released from the law, having died to that which held us captive" (v. 6). We have died, and as far as the law's ability to captivate and enslave us, we are gloriously deceased. We are no longer slaves; we are not slaves to sin, because we are no longer slaves to the law. The power of the law has been completely abrogated.

To change the metaphor a bit, after Lincoln's Emancipation Proclamation in 1863, slaves who were once under the law of slavery were immediately freed. The law that permitted slavery had been abrogated by the federal law that made slave ownership illegal. In the same way, we have been emancipated from the law's dominion. We are no longer slaves for one simple reason: the law no longer has power over us. It cannot engender sin in us; it cannot condemn us. We are free, we are dead—and yet we live. We've been emancipated.

Of course, this freedom and death do not mean that we can live in selfishness and laziness. On the contrary, what this freedom does is enable us to "serve in the new way of the Spirit and not in the old way of the written code" (v. 6). Do you see the contrast here between the *new way* of the Spirit and the *old way* of the written code? What Paul calls the "old way of the written code" is simply the law as it was first delivered in the Mosaic commands on Mount Sinai. It is that old written code, those ten words or commandments that we never fully obey, that we've died to. The old way of the written code produced sin and was a way of drudgery. It was a law that did not originate from within our own hearts but was imposed on us from without. It was a law written on cold, dead, stone tablets.

The new way of the Spirit is a way of voluntary service, engendered by the work of the Holy Spirit from within hearts that have been made alive. Jeremiah foretold this transformation:

> Behold, the days are coming, declares the Lord, when I will make a new covenant with the house of Israel and the house of Judah. . . . I will put my law within them, and I will write it on their hearts. And I will be their God, and they shall be my people. . . . For I will forgive their iniquity, and I will remember their sin no more." (Jer. 31:31–34)

The prophet Ezekiel echoed a similar thought:

> I will sprinkle clean water on you, and you shall be clean from all your uncleannesses, and from all your idols I will cleanse you. And I will give you a new heart, and a new spirit I will put within you. And I will remove the heart of stone from your flesh and give you a heart of flesh. And I will put my Spirit within you, and cause you to walk in my statutes and be careful to obey my rules. (Ezek. 36:25–27)

We've been freed to serve in the "new way of the Spirit," a way that originates in hearts that have been transformed by the gracious pronouncement, "You are righteous." Because of the gospel, God's prior work on our behalf, the Spirit has written the law upon our hearts, and we're no longer obligated to obey it as a way to earn God's benediction. Instead, we freely desire to serve him out of gratitude for the new life we've been given.

I opened this chapter talking about the draft and how those who are dead are free from the Selective Service System requirements. In the United States we now have an all-volunteer military. No one is forced into the military; men and women freely join. Even though all males have to register, no one is forced to serve.

That's the kind of military the church has. Do we serve? Yes, of course. But not because we are forced to by unwelcome pressure from without. We serve because the Holy Spirit indwells us and we're new. We have a new desire, a new inner law that commands us to love as we have been loved. We have the indwelling power of the Holy Spirit and we're freed from trying to earn our Father's love and welcome. We're gloriously dead and even more gloriously alive!

Day 27

Holy and Righteous and Good

So the law is holy, and the commandment is holy and righteous and good. —Romans 7:12

After everything I have said about the law and our response to it, you might be wondering how we should think about God's law. Is the law intrinsically flawed? Should we denigrate it or despise it? Should we relegate it to an ancient religion, an old, out-of-date covenant? Should we wink at it and just say, "That was for then, but this is for now"? In other words, does the spectacular beauty of grace make the law worthless and ugly?

Paul anticipated these questions, so he penned these words extolling the virtue of the law: "The law is holy, and the commandment is holy and righteous and good." No, God's rules are not flawed in any way, as David wrote in Psalm 19:7: "The law of the LORD is perfect." He wrote that it is not only perfect (complete, without blemish, blameless), but also that it is sure, right, pure, clean, true, righteous, more valuable than gold, and delicious. It is efficacious, which means it has the ability to warn us about how to live, and it promises blessing for those who keep it. In Psalm 1, we learn about the blessings of the man who delights in and meditates on the law, and in Psalm 119 we hear the heart's cry of the person who loves it:

Oh that my ways may be steadfast
in keeping your statutes! (v. 5)

With my whole heart I seek you;
let me not wander from your commandments! (v. 10)

Blessed are you, O LORD;
  teach me your statutes! (v. 12)

Open my eyes, that I may behold
  wondrous things out of your law. (v. 18)

I will run the way of your commandments
  when you enlarge my heart! (v. 32)

Lead me in the path of your commandments,
  for I delight in it. (v. 35)

You are good and do good;
  teach me your statutes. (v. 68)

Your hands have made and fashioned me;
  give me understanding that I may learn your commandments.
    (v. 73)

Hold me up, that I may be safe
  and have regard for your statutes continually! (v. 117)

I am your servant; give me understanding,
  that I may know your testimonies! (v. 125)

Make your face shine upon your servant,
  and teach me your statutes.
My eyes shed streams of tears
  because people do not keep your law. (vv. 135–36)

I long for your salvation, O LORD,
  and your law is my delight.
Let my soul live and praise you,
  and let your rules help me.
I have gone astray like a lost sheep; seek your servant,
  for I do not forget your commandments. (vv. 174–76)

Even before the new covenant was established, even before grace was made plain at Calvary, Old Testament saints realized that although the law was holy and righteous and good, they were unable to keep it without direct intervention from its Author. Our heart's cry should echo theirs: "Oh Lord, your law is beautiful, but you must transform me in order for me to even begin to keep it!"

The law itself is beautiful because it is a reflection on the character of God, and his character is beautiful. "As holy, just, and good it reflects the character of God and is the transcript of his perfection."[47] The law is a *transcript* of God's perfections. It tells us what he is like. It helps us see the unseen—what is Jehovah like? He is perfect, holy, good, loving, and righteous, and fellowship with him is the most desirable relationship one might have.

> As "holy" the commandment reflects the transcendence and purity of God and demands of us the correspondent consecration and purity; as "righteous" it reflects the equity of God and exacts of us in its demand and sanction nothing but that which is equitable; as "good" it promotes man's highest well-being and thus expresses the goodness of God.[48]

We love the law because the law tells us of our God. But we cannot obey it.

Paul teaches us that the problem we have with the law flows out of hearts infected with sin. As an example from his own life, he uses the commandment against coveting. He writes that his struggle with coveting had its origin in his sinful heart, that when he heard the command "You shall not covet," the sin within him seized an opportunity and "produced" in him "all kinds of covetousness" (Rom. 7:7–8). He asks, "Did that which is good [the law], then, bring death to me? By no means! It was sin, producing death in me through what is good" (v. 13). And here finally we've come to our core problem:

> For we know that the law is spiritual, but I am of the flesh, sold under sin. For I do not understand my own actions. For I do not do what I want, but I do the very thing I hate. (vv. 14–15)

Imagine, if you will, two outwardly righteous men praying Psalm 119. Both of them love God and see him portrayed in the beauty of his law. Both of them are serious about obedience and long with everything within them to obey. Both of them pray every morning that their lives might be a reflection of his nature and that their inner motives and outer deeds would bring great glory to their God.

One of them ends the day in despair, saying, "I do not understand my own actions. For I do not do what I want, but I do the very thing I hate" (Rom. 7:15). The other affirms, "I always do the things that are pleasing to him" (John 8:29). One confesses, "I do not do the good that I want, but the evil I do not want is what I keep on doing" (Rom. 7:19). The other declares, "My food is to do the will of him who sent me and to accomplish his work" (John 4:34). The first man says, "So I find it to be a law that when I want to do right, evil lies close at hand. For I delight in the law of God, in my inner being, but I see in my members another law" (Rom. 7:21–23). The second one utters, "Behold I have come to do your will, O God" (Heb. 10:7) and enters into the last hours of his life, breathing out these words: "My Father, if it be possible, let this cup pass from me; nevertheless, not as I will, but as you will. . . . My Father, if this cannot pass unless I drink it, your will be done" (Matt. 26:39, 42).

Can you see? Paul, an anointed apostle who loved the law and longed to obey it, found that it produced despair in him. The Lord Jesus, who also loved the law from the time he was a child and always lived in complete submission to it, even when it cost him his reputation for being righteous, obeyed it to the end.

So then, what is our attitude toward the law? We love it. We pray that we will obey it. We long to reflect the marvelous character of our Father, *and we rest wholly in the imputed righteousness of the only One who ever fulfilled it.*

BLESSED WRETCHEDNESS

*Wretched man that I am! Who will deliver me from this body of
death? Thanks be to God through Jesus Christ our Lord!*
—Romans 7:24–25

The Lord Jesus lived in complete submission to the law of God. His
obedience was not mere outward compliance. His obedience was
completely perfect because it was motivated by a heart completely
devoted to glorifying his Father. When he obeyed, he didn't obey like
we sometimes do—hoping that our obedience will make us feel better
about ourselves, hoping that if we obey we'll earn the respect of others
or merit blessing from God.

No, his obedience was always selfless and thoroughly loving. It
was focused solely on one thing: loving God with his whole heart,
soul, mind, and strength and his neighbor as himself. He loved perfectly and prayed continually that his Father's will would be done
through him because he loved nothing more than pleasing him.

Jesus was the quintessential embodiment of the godly man in
Psalm 1. That righteous man delights in the law of the Lord, and "on
his law he meditates day and night" (v. 2). He is happy, like a fruitful,
luxurious tree, planted by refreshing streams of water. In all that he
does, he prospers. He is truly blessed, because God showers him with
his favor.

Jesus never walked in the "counsel of the wicked" (Psalm 1:1).
When Peter tried to counsel him against going to Jerusalem to die,
Jesus rebuked him, "Get behind me, Satan! You are a hindrance to
me. For you are not setting your mind on the things of God, but on the
things of man" (Matt. 16:23).

He didn't "stand in the way of sinners" nor "sit in the seat of scoff-
ers" (Ps. 1:1). He didn't take up a position that embraced rebellion or

autonomy. He didn't scoff or mock or brag. He never delighted in sin or rejoiced in wrongdoing.

What did he delight in? The law of the Lord, of course. He found pleasure in knowing and obeying the law of God. It made him absolutely happy to please the Father he loved. To him, the law was the most precious, most costly treasure in life. He valued it above all things—above his reputation, the love and respect of his family, the approbation of the crowds, or his own personal comfort and well-being. He was the personification of the Psalm 1 man.

What are the promises given to the man who loves God's law like this? "He is like a tree planted by streams of water that yields its fruit in its season and its leaf does not wither. In all that he does, he prospers" (Ps. 1:3).

He is blessed. But is that what we see when we look at the life of the Savior? Do we see a man who looks like he's blessed and prospering? Doesn't his life (and particularly the final years of his life) more closely resemble "chaff that the wind drives away"? (Ps. 1:4). He stands before the judgment and is found guilty. He is expelled from the congregation of the righteous. He doesn't prosper. He's accused of blasphemy. On Calvary he is forsaken, not vindicated. His way perishes.

How are we to make sense of this? How are we to integrate the blessings promised to the man of Psalm 1 and the testimony of the life of someone who suffers for being righteous? We understand when we hear Paul's desperate confession and plea and then believe when we hear God's earth-shaking answer.

> Wretched man that I am! Who will deliver me from this body of death? Thanks be to God through Jesus Christ our Lord! (Rom. 7:24–25)

Do you love God's law? Let me rephrase that. Do you wish that you loved God's law and longed to obey it all the time and with your whole heart? When you're thinking straight do you want nothing more than to know that you've brought glory to your Father? Me too. But then there is my life. There is the unbelief, the selfishness, the incessant realization that I always fall short. Oh, the wretchedness and misery I have lived in—never being perfectly obedient, always failing to love in some way.

When Paul cries out that he is wretched, he isn't using hyperbole. He is truly miserable, distressed, and suffering. He is despairing because he can never find a place of rest for his conscience. He has learned from experience that all his efforts at righteousness fall short. Even his good works are nothing, are rubbish, because the righteousness he longs to possess is always beyond his grasp.

Like Paul, we need a deliverer. We need someone who will be righteous in our place and deliver us from our relentless failure and dominating slavery to sin. We need someone to come and rescue us and bestow upon us something we could never earn: a record of full obedience. We need to be "found" in Christ, "not having a righteousness of [our] own that comes from the law, but that which comes through faith in Christ, the righteousness from God that depends on faith" (Phil. 3:9).

Oh, praise God! Jesus Christ is our deliverer. He is the one whose earthly life was marked by suffering and ultimate judgment. He became the worthless chaff battered by the fierce wind of God's judgment so that we could be the luxuriant fruitful tree, planted by cooling streams. He knew of a tree, too, but it wasn't the tree of Psalm 1. It was the tree of Golgotha where he was forsaken so that we would be qualified to hear the blessed benediction of a smiling God forever, no matter how we fail.

> The LORD bless you and keep you;
> the LORD make his face to shine upon you and be gracious to you;
> the LORD lift up his countenance upon you and give you peace.
>   (Num. 6:24–26)

He wasn't blessed; he was cursed: "Christ redeemed us from the curse by becoming a curse for us" (Gal. 3:13). He wasn't kept from harm but rather, "it was the will of the LORD to crush him" (Isa. 53:10). The Father whom he loved with more love than we could ever imagine looked upon his Son, and his Son saw something in his Father's gaze that he had never seen before: darkness and wrath. He was "smitten by God and afflicted" (Isa. 53:4). The Father turned away from him in his deepest hour of desperation, and the Son was left bereft of the smile that had gladdened him throughout eternity. God the Father took the blessing of peace from God the Son so that he could give it to you.

Think of it. Because we believe, we've been given *all* the blessings that the Son earned by his obedience. In the resurrection we've been set free from the power of sin, and the words of God's blessing have been forever spoken over our lives. What blessed wretchedness! What glorious deliverance! Complete righteousness and freedom is ours today. Who will deliver us? Jesus Christ our Lord! Of course, the Father has at last

> highly exalted him and bestowed upon him the name that is above every name, so that at the name of Jesus every knee should bow, in heaven and on earth and under the earth, and every tongue confess that Jesus Christ is Lord, to the glory of God the Father (Phil. 2:9–11)

Now he's the flourishing tree who produces glorious fruit in our lives; now he's receiving all the praise that he deserved all along. In your glorious wretchedness today, praise him! Praise him that he's your deliverer, and even though you still fail miserably, praise him that you're completely blessed.

Day 29

No Condemnation—
No, Not Now, Not Ever

There is therefore now no condemnation for those who are in Christ Jesus. —Romans 8:1

Here we are at Romans 8 at last, one of the best-loved, most well-known passages in the entire Bible, and my personal favorite. I'm so happy that our final four days will be spent delving into the truths presented here, but before we start, particularly because this chapter is so familiar, perhaps you'll take a moment to read it (if your Bible isn't close by you can read it in Appendix 1) and pray that the Spirit will enlighten your eyes to the work of the Holy Spirit in the lives of those who are in Christ.

Paul begins this gracious chapter with the word "therefore," or "in light of all the preceding." In doing this he is reminding us of all he's written thus far. So let's walk again down the path we've traveled so that we can enjoy the full force of the words now before us.

In Romans 1 we learned that we are "loved by God and called to be saints" (v. 7). We have been given salvation through belief in the gospel, a gospel that reveals the righteousness of God and declares that "the righteous shall live by faith" (vv. 16–17).

In Romans 2 we were reminded that those who obey God's law will receive glory, honor, and peace, and, conversely, those who disobey will receive wrath and fury (vv. 6–12). We learned that true obedience is inward and accomplished by the work of the Spirit, not by outward compliance to religious ritual.

Next we learned that though we are all sinners, and none of us obeys perfectly, the righteousness of God has been manifested apart from the law through faith in Jesus Christ for all who believe (3:21–22).

God justifies or declares righteous those who put their trust in Jesus Christ (vv. 28–30).

In Romans 4 we were reminded of the faith of Abraham, who was declared justified apart from his works by his simple belief (v. 9) that God is loving and faithful to his word. Because we've been justified apart from our works, we no longer have an obligation to obey the law to earn merit, and we are no longer under the curse brought about by our transgression of it (v. 15).

We saw that Romans 5 opens with the statement that God no longer has any wrath left for us because we've been justified by faith. He is at peace with us (v. 1), and that gift of peace was given to us while we were still weak, ungodly, and sinful (vv. 6–8). Through the obedience of one Man, true righteousness has been earned for all of us, and with that true righteousness came eternal life (vv. 18–19). The perfect obedience of the incarnate God brings great comfort to our souls.

"Remember who you are" is the message of Romans 6, where we find the first imperative or obligation: "So, you also must consider yourselves dead to sin and alive to God in Christ Jesus" (v. 11). Because we are now justified, we are no longer under the law as a way to curry favor or add to our good record with God. We are not under law but under grace, and it is that very grace, when properly understood, that will impel true obedience (vv. 14–15).

Paul's struggle against the sin in his own heart and his reassurance of our freedom from both guilt and sin's demands is the topic of Romans 7, which ends with blessed wretchedness and the declaration that deliverance has come through Jesus Christ our Lord, even to those who continue to struggle with sin.

Now, at last we come to the magnificent declaration of Romans 8:

There is therefore now no condemnation for those who are in Christ Jesus.

Oh, think of it! If your affections aren't moved right now, if you're feeling like this is just sort of ho-hum, more of the same yada-yada gospel, please stop right now and beg the Spirit to work in you. It is this truth of freedom from condemnation that will fuel your obedience and set you ablaze with love for him.

Because of all that God has done for us in Christ, because of Christ's incarnation, perfect obedience, substitutionary death, bodily resurrection, and ascension, we who were once under God's sentence of condemnation and death have been completely set free. We have been loved!

> In this is love, not that we have loved God but that he loved us and sent his Son to be the propitiation for our sins. (1 John 4:10)

Jesus Christ is our propitiation. What *propitiation* means is to make an atoning sacrifice for another. Jesus is our wrath bearer. In his person he received the entire weight of *all* God's wrath for *all* our sin. In three hours he received *all* the wrath we would have known had we spent an eternity in hell. *All* of God's wrath for *all* of our sin—not just the sin that we committed before we came to Christ, not just the sin that we have committed since our conversion, or not even just the sins we've committed today. He received God's wrath for the sins we will commit tomorrow and through all of our tomorrows until we finally die. He paid for *all* our sin. We will never be recipients of God's wrath and condemnation because he's already borne it all.

> If Jesus bore all of God's wrath for all of your sin,
> how much wrath does God have left for you?

The answer is none. Go ahead and believe that. Say it out loud: "God has no wrath left for me!" Believe it. Jesus Christ has fully, irrevocably, unequivocally, and freely granted you freedom from all the wrath you deserve.

Are you struggling with that a bit? Here's one helpful way to look at it: would God be a good or a wicked parent if he punished you for your sin more than once? Do you punish your children for the same sin over and over again? I hope not. God already punished all of our sin when he punished his Son in our place. And now that we are "in

Christ Jesus" he will never punish him or us again. You are now completely free from even the threat of punishment.

In case that's not enough to get you smiling and stunned in awe by his love, here's another thought: when you read that there is now no condemnation, it's easy to think, *Okay, that means that right now, as I've read this, there is no condemnation, but there used to be.* But when we reason that way, we're forgetting that this "now" was written two thousand years ago. In fact, for us who have been chosen by God, *there never was any condemnation; it was all handled on our behalf from before the beginning of time.*

Think of it: Ephesians tells us that Jesus was slain before the foundation of the world (Eph. 1:4). And God "saved us and called us to a holy calling, not because of our works but because of his own purpose and grace, *which he gave us in Christ Jesus before the ages began*" (2 Tim. 1:9). Before the worlds began God looked down through time and chose to free you from condemnation. He gave you grace and poured out upon you his love before you ever took one breath. Oh, glorious freedom!

Rejoice my sister, my brother, today. You never were under condemnation because he took care of it all in eternity past. You've been set completely free, and there is *now* no condemnation hanging over your life. Will you allow yourself to live in that freedom and rejoice today?

Day 30

ALL THINGS

And we know that for those who love God all things work together for good, for those who are called according to his purpose. For those whom he foreknew he also predestined to be conformed to the image of his Son, in order that he might be the firstborn among many brothers. And those whom he predestined he also called, and those whom he called he also justified, and those whom he justified he also glorified. —Romans 8:28–30

Because we live in a world blighted by sin, life here is frequently not what we wish it would be. My life is the same as yours—just because I am a writer, public speaker, and counselor doesn't mean that I don't walk through trials like you do.

In November 2010, my dear eighty-eight-year-old mother was diagnosed with stage 3 breast cancer and has since undergone surgery and radiation. Phil's mother, a woman who poured out her life for missions and the church, has slipped into the vacuity of geriatric dementia, while his wonderful father, a man who was always "working over at the church," is no longer able to walk.

In January 2011, my husband was unexpectedly and supposedly permanently laid off from the job where he had worked for over three decades. We immediately downsized, moving to a very rural portion of our county, nearer our church, only to have him rehired five months later. He then had to make the commute three days a week. We lost the joy we'd experienced in our former home, which had been the center of family gatherings, because the new home was small and too far from the rest of the family. The family began to gather at my daughter's house, and while I was glad that she was able to host them, I felt isolated, obsolete, and humiliated.

On any number of occasions I wondered about God's purpose in all that. How was this something good? How did these changes advance the kingdom or make our lives better? We had prayed about the downsizing move; why didn't God close the door? After all, he knew that Phil was going to be rehired.

I admit that I didn't respond well to much of that trial, but I was finally able to ask myself, what did I learn from it all? The answer that resounds in my heart is, "I am a great sinner but I have a great Savior." I can't look back on that year and say, "My, what a good girl I was." All I can say is that I am more fully resting now in the completely sufficient righteousness of Another. The End.

I know that many of you are probably going through difficulties that make my little season of trial seem like a cakewalk. I am satisfied that the Lord knows exactly what kinds of trials each of us needs to walk through to accomplish his goals. I am also convinced that the Lord uses everything in our lives for one good purpose: that we would be conformed to the image of his Son, "in order that he might be the firstborn among many brothers" (v. 29).

Even though I still don't have a clear understanding of God's purposes in my immediate trials, I do understand at least one thing: he is working in my character to change me; he's making me aware of idols in my heart, of unbelief and false gods. He's doing a deep and painful yet beneficial work in my life.

To begin with, I was blind before to many of the weaknesses that I've become acutely aware of over the last year. For instance, I didn't know how much of my identity was tied up in my house and my ability to host my family and friends. When all that the house represented to me was taken away, I struggled to see my identity as hidden in Christ and as one completely loved. Frankly, the fact that God loved me didn't matter as it should have. I wanted to be able to look at my house and my hospitality and feel proud. I loved having people over and feeling well heeled. I loved decorating for Christmas and hearing the ohs and ahs when people came into my house.

In moving us to less than half the square footage of our former home, the Lord forced me to give up many of the things that I had become tied to and loved. Although I was glad to be rid of some of the junk, I wept over the loss of my library.

In addition, I've come to see how I idolized convenience and the ability to pop around the corner to my favorite stores in less than five minutes. I loved being able to spend money easily, when I wanted to spend it and at the stores I wanted to spend it in. After the move, it took me a good thirty minutes to get to my favorite grocery stores. I had loved the convenience of a restaurant on every corner and a Starbucks whenever I was in the mood. After the move, we talked about "going into town."

Also, I had been completely unaware of how deeply I had bought into the youth, happening, fun culture of the beach and Southern California. After the move, I became part of a rural retirement community where yesterday is more important than tomorrow and the primary amusements include bingo, Bunco, and golf. I looked down on and judged some whose lives seemed to consist of nothing more than gossip, playing games, and making sure that everyone else obeyed the rules.

In light of all this disturbing self-awareness, the imputed righteousness of Christ has become sweeter to me. During that time he began to teach me how to be patient, how to love the things of God, and how to love neighbors with whom I think I have nothing in common (I flatter myself). I'm learning what it means to be hidden in Christ. This is a great good.

This is my hope today, that he who foreknew, predestined, called, justified, and, yes, even glorified me, will be faithful to continue his work in my life. All the trials and suffering that we go through are focused ultimately on one goal: that we would be transformed and become like our elder Brother. We do not see how enslaved and deceived we still are; we do not see how our protestations of love for God are something else entirely. But he does, so he works all things for good, that we will become what he has declared we already are: justified and, yes, even glorified. "And I am sure of this, that he who began a good work in you will bring it to completion at the day of Jesus Christ" (Phil. 1:6). Rest in his work.

If God Is for Us

What then shall we say to these things? If God is for us, who can be against us? He who did not spare his own Son but gave him up for us all, how will he not also with him graciously give us all things? Who shall bring any charge against God's elect? It is God who justifies. Who is to condemn? Christ Jesus is the one who died—more than that, who was raised—who is at the right hand of God, who indeed is interceding for us. —Romans 8:31–34

We've spent a month soaking our soul in the glorious truths of the gospel. What will our response be? Will we finally believe that God is for us? In case you're still not convinced, here are more gospel words: he did not spare his own Son but gave him up for us.

He didn't spare his own Son but gave him up for you. This Son is the Son he loved, the Beloved, in whom he was well pleased. God's giving up of his Son didn't begin at Calvary or even at Bethlehem. He gave him up for us from the beginning of time, from the first moment after the covenant of redemption was agreed upon. From before the ages began, from before the foundation of the world, the Father had already determined to give up the Son for you. We cannot even begin to know what that giving up was like for our Father. He gave up his one precious Son so that he might gain millions of adopted children.

In arguing from the greater to the lesser, Paul is seeking to encourage his readers:

> Listen! If he was willing to do that, to give up the Son he loved, why would you ever doubt his willingness to graciously give you everything you need? He's promised to care for you and to carry you all the way home. Why would you doubt?

Paul anticipates the source of our doubts about God's continued welcome and acceptance of us. Our enemy Satan has one goal in mind: he wants to make us doubt that God loves us and loves to graciously give us everything. He wants to kill our faith and make us think that our loving Father is like Pharaoh, demanding that we make bricks without straw.

How does Satan do this? How does he kill our faith and veil God's love for us? He reminds us, and those around us, of our failures. He enflames our enemies and provokes them to point out our sin. Are you being persecuted for your failures by anyone? The voice behind their voice is Satan's. He also hisses half-truths into our conscience, pointing out our failures, incessantly reminding us of every sin, arousing that inner slave driver to mercilessly apply the whip of the law to us. But he doesn't stop there. John saw him for who he was, the one who had the audacity to accuse us before the Father who gave up his Son for us.

> And I heard a loud voice in heaven, saying, "Now the salvation and the power and the kingdom of our God and the authority of his Christ have come, for the accuser of our brothers has been thrown down, who accuses them day and night before our God." (Rev. 12:10)

Do you want to know where that crushing, damnable accusation comes from? It doesn't come from the Holy Spirit. Yes, the Spirit does convict us of sin (I outlined some of that in yesterday's reading), but the Spirit doesn't tell us that God is angry or that he doesn't love us or that now we've finally blown it so badly that we'll never get back to where we were. That's not the Spirit. That hopelessness isn't the voice of God. That's the enemy. If the voice you hear draws you back into yourself, back into trying to prove you are really serious about being holy, you can know that this is not your Father speaking. It's the father of lies (John 8:44), who would love nothing better than to make you hate and distrust the God who gave up his Son for you. Here's how you can answer him: "It is God who justifies. He elected me. He chose me. He justifies me."

Who will condemn us? No one! And that is because Jesus Christ is the one who died for the sin that would have condemned. Culpability for our sin is gone, obliterated, and because of God's loving election, the condemnation due us because of sin is obliterated too. He will never condemn us now, because the Son died and took our condemnation. But that's not all. Not only did the Beloved die; he was also raised for us. Again, his resurrection means that we are justified: our record is not simply that we have never sinned but that we have always obeyed. Why would God turn from us in our hour of need, when his records show that we've always been completely righteous?

Oh, and if all this is not enough, here's more good news: this Jesus, the Beloved Son, is right now in heaven, sitting at the position of power at the Father's right hand, ruling and overruling everything in our lives to accomplish his purpose of loving us and making us more and more happy. He is there interceding for us. He is praying for us and standing with us before the Holy God.

When the Accuser comes in to make an accusation about you and how you've blown it once again, our advocate, our defense attorney, Jesus Christ the righteous (1 John 2:1), doesn't let him get one word out. He presents before the Father the list of all his own righteousnesses and holds out nail-pierced hands and tells the Accuser to shut his lying mouth. He casts him and his lies down and then turns to the Father and prays that our faith will not fail.

Dear sister, dear brother, hear the life-giving, faith-sustaining Word speak to you: no one can condemn you. No one can make God stop loving you. No one can say anything about you that will in any way diminish his love for you. Now that you are his (and, really, in God's perspective you always were), nothing you can do will thwart his desire to graciously give you all things.

God is for us. No one can stand against us or accuse us or bring a charge against us or condemn us or stop our Savior from protecting, pardoning, and interceding for us. No one. Not Satan, not your human enemies, not your own unbelieving heart. No one.

And even if you struggle to fully believe this today, even your struggle won't separate you from his purpose to bless you, because the Son has believed in your place. Look away from yourself. Look away from your faith or faithful obedience. Look to the faithful, obedient Son instead. Transfer all your trust to him and know that God is for us because we are his, just as God the Father is for God the Son because he is his.

Day 32

NOTHING CAN SEPARATE
US FROM GOD'S LOVE

For I am sure that neither death nor life, nor angels nor rulers, nor things present nor things to come, nor powers, nor height nor depth, nor anything else in all creation, will be able to separate us from the love of God in Christ Jesus our Lord. —Romans 8:38–39

From the very beginning of time, God determined to love us. He knew all about our sin—our unbelief, our pride, our idolatry, our fear, and our selfishness. Still, he determined to love us and make us his own. He knew about our sin before it existed, and yet it pleased him to create a world like ours and rule sovereignly over Adam's fall so that his mercy and the love and perfection of his Son would be celebrated. God was not the author of that dreadful sin, but he ruled sovereignly over it in order to accomplish all his good will and gain glory for himself.

Our sin will not separate us from God's love, because his love was predetermined before we sinned, and even our sin functions to make his love look more glorious.

We are completely, thoroughly, fully, and freely known and loved and completely free to rest in that love. Suspend your unbelief. Silence your inner slave driver. Allow yourself one minute of ecstasy. He *will* love you. He will have you for his own. He will draw you near to himself. He will bless you. Enjoy his love. Receive it. Relish it. Delight in it. Dance!

Listen to all the negatives that Paul uses to make his point about the never-ending-ness of the Father's love: neither death, nor life, nor angels, nor rulers, nor things present, nor things to come, nor powers, nor height, nor depth, nor anything else in all creation will be able to separate us from God's love. If I were Paul's editor, I would have insisted that he clump all those "nors" into a more concise list, but that's not what the Spirit had in mind. The Spirit wants to blow your mind, to shake you up, to move you out of your apathetic complacency and cringing fear and self-absorption. He wants to overwhelm you, because otherwise you'll continue to navel-gaze and list-make and try to pull the wagon of your self-improvement on down the glory road to the nirvana of self-approval. So he piles it on, redundantly, over and over again, trying to shake you free and loose you from all that you think you know about how love works.

> Neither, nor, nor, nor, nor, nor, nor, nor, nor, nor anything else in all creation will be able to separate us from the love of God in Christ Jesus our Lord.

Ten times "nor"—ten times. The Spirit finishes this list with ". . . and in case you try to cram something else onto the list that you think I missed, not that either." Perhaps you will read this aloud with me now, praying that the Spirit will grant you grace to believe:

> When I die, while I am here dying daily, I will not be separated from him. No matter what happens when I face death, no matter how my faith may waver, I will never be separated from him as I walk through that dark river, and his loving hand will draw me up from those waters and his arms will embrace me.

> While I live, nothing can separate me from his love. On the days that I forget him, on the days when I doubt, on the days when I rejoice and believe, nothing will separate me from his love and nothing will affect his love for me in any way.

> There is no angel—not Lucifer, not any seen or unseen spiritual being—who has more power than the power of God's love. Satan cannot tempt me to sin in such a way that I will be cut off from God's love, nor can he accuse me or point out my sin in such a way that it will make God stop loving me.

> There is no ruler—political or spiritual or otherwise—that has the authority to cut me off from God's love. They can all make all the pronouncements they want. They can say that God is dead and

that I cannot worship him. They can assign me to the depth of the earth's dungeons, and there I will find the sweetest of wines from the hands of the Savior, who loves me and suffers with me.

There is nothing in existence now in this entire universe that is able to separate me from the love of God in Christ Jesus. Not cell phones, oak trees, oceans, stock markets, microbes, bacteria, political movements, faithless churches, powerful cults, or sin—mine nor others'—that can separate me from his love.

Nothing that exists in this entire universe will be able to separate me from the love of God in Christ Jesus. There is no sin, no temptation, no trial, no disaster, no election, no bank failure, no sickness, no treachery, no debauchery, no darkness, and "no pit so deep that God's love is not deeper still."[49]

There is no political, military, monetary, or ecclesiastical power and, most importantly, no willpower (not mine or others') that will ever be powerful enough to overcome and defeat God's commitment to love me forever.

There is no ruler over or above this earth that is able to separate me from God's love. There is nothing invisible, nothing in the heavens, and nothing on any planet or star or nebula that is more powerful than God's love.

There is nothing beneath this earth, not all the power of hell itself, that will ever be able to defeat God's love for me. Hell's gates crumble when assaulted by a fierce love like this.

And just in case anything has been missed, just in case I can think of something or have a suspicion that I've missed something, there is *nothing else* in all creation—*nothing else*—that will be able to separate me from the love of God in Christ Jesus our Lord.

Have you heard the good news? Do you know that you are loved? Has he made you sure? If not, then pray now that you would be.

In all our trials—in tribulation, distress, persecution, famine, nakedness, danger, sword, and martyrdom—we are more than conquerors because we are beloved sons and daughters with whom he is well pleased, and because he loves us he turns everything—even suffering and death—into good. We are not at the mercy of anything in the universe. And even in our death we have victory, because death itself has been swallowed up in the life of the love of the Father.

> This is great news. This is the best news you've ever heard. You can bank on this news. It is the sure word of God to you. "I love you. I always have. I always will." Believe and rejoice in that love!

Appendix 1

Romans 8

There is therefore now no condemnation for those who are in Christ Jesus. For the law of the Spirit of life has set you free in Christ Jesus from the law of sin and death. For God has done what the law, weakened by the flesh, could not do. By sending his own Son in the likeness of sinful flesh and for sin, he condemned sin in the flesh, in order that the righteous requirement of the law might be fulfilled in us, who walk not according to the flesh but according to the Spirit. For those who live according to the flesh set their minds on the things of the flesh, but those who live according to the Spirit set their minds on the things of the Spirit. For to set the mind on the flesh is death, but to set the mind on the Spirit is life and peace. For the mind that is set on the flesh is hostile to God, for it does not submit to God's law; indeed, it cannot. Those who are in the flesh cannot please God.

You, however, are not in the flesh but in the Spirit, if in fact the Spirit of God dwells in you. Anyone who does not have the Spirit of Christ does not belong to him. But if Christ is in you, although the body is dead because of sin, the Spirit is life because of righteousness. If the Spirit of him who raised Jesus from the dead dwells in you, he who raised Christ Jesus from the dead will also give life to your mortal bodies through his Spirit who dwells in you.

So then, brothers, we are debtors, not to the flesh, to live according to the flesh. For if you live according to the flesh you will die, but if by the Spirit you put to death the deeds of the body, you will live. For all who are led by the Spirit of God are sons of God. For you did not receive the spirit of slavery to fall back into fear, but you have received the Spirit of adoption as sons, by whom we cry, "Abba! Father!" The Spirit himself bears witness with our spirit that we are children of

God, and if children, then heirs—heirs of God and fellow heirs with Christ, provided we suffer with him in order that we may also be glorified with him.

For I consider that the sufferings of this present time are not worth comparing with the glory that is to be revealed to us. For the creation waits with eager longing for the revealing of the sons of God. For the creation was subjected to futility, not willingly, but because of him who subjected it, in hope that the creation itself will be set free from its bondage to corruption and obtain the freedom of the glory of the children of God. For we know that the whole creation has been groaning together in the pains of childbirth until now. And not only the creation, but we ourselves, who have the firstfruits of the Spirit, groan inwardly as we wait eagerly for adoption as sons, the redemption of our bodies. For in this hope we were saved. Now hope that is seen is not hope. For who hopes for what he sees? But if we hope for what we do not see, we wait for it with patience.

Likewise the Spirit helps us in our weakness. For we do not know what to pray for as we ought, but the Spirit himself intercedes for us with groanings too deep for words. And he who searches hearts knows what is the mind of the Spirit, because the Spirit intercedes for the saints according to the will of God. And we know that for those who love God all things work together for good, for those who are called according to his purpose. For those whom he foreknew he also predestined to be conformed to the image of his Son, in order that he might be the firstborn among many brothers. And those whom he predestined he also called, and those whom he called he also justified, and those whom he justified he also glorified.

What then shall we say to these things? If God is for us, who can be against us? He who did not spare his own Son but gave him up for us all, how will he not also with him graciously give us all things? Who shall bring any charge against God's elect? It is God who justifies. Who is to condemn? Christ Jesus is the one who died—more than that, who was raised—who is at the right hand of God, who indeed is interceding for us. Who shall separate us from the love of Christ?

Shall tribulation, or distress, or persecution, or famine, or nakedness, or danger, or sword? As it is written,

> "For your sake we are being killed all the day long;
>   we are regarded as sheep to be slaughtered."

No, in all these things we are more than conquerors through him who loved us. For I am sure that neither death nor life, nor angels nor rulers, nor things present nor things to come, nor powers, nor height nor depth, nor anything else in all creation, will be able to separate us from the love of God in Christ Jesus our Lord.

Appendix 2

The Most Important Good News

I (Elyse) didn't begin to understand the gospel until the summer before my twenty-first birthday. Although I had attended church from time to time in my childhood, I'll admit that it never really transformed me in any significant way. I was frequently taken to Sunday school where I heard stories about Jesus. I knew, without really understanding, the importance of Christmas and Easter. I remember looking at the beautiful stained-glass windows, with their cranberry red and deep cerulean blue, that depicted Jesus knocking on a garden door, and having a vague sense that being religious was good. But I didn't have the foggiest idea about the gospel.

When adolescence came barging in, my strongest memories are those of despair and anger. I was consistently in trouble, and I hated everyone who pointed that out. There were nights when I prayed that I would be good or, more specifically, get out of whatever trouble I was in and do better, only to be disappointed and angered by the failures of the following day.

Upon graduation from high school at seventeen, I got married, had a baby, and was divorced all before the third decade of my life began. It was during the following months and years that I discovered the anesthetizing effects of drugs, alcohol, and illicit relationships. Although I would have been known as a girl who liked to party, I was utterly lost and joyless, and I was beginning to know it.

At one point, I can remember telling a friend that I felt like I was fifty years old, which, at that point in my life, was the oldest I could imagine anyone being. I was exhausted and disgusted, so I decided to set about improving myself. I worked a full-time job, took a full load at a local junior college, and cared for my son. I changed my living arrangements and tried to start over. I didn't know that the Holy Spirit was working in my heart, calling me to the Son. I just knew that something had to change. Don't misunderstand: I was still living a shamefully wicked life; it's just that I felt that I was beginning to wake up to something different.

At this point, Julie entered my life. She was my next-door neighbor, and she was a Christian. She was kind to me, and we became fast friends. She had a quality of life about her that attracted me, and she was always talking to me about her Savior, Jesus. She let me know that she was praying for me and would frequently encourage me to "get saved." Although I'd had that Sunday school training, what she had to say was something completely different from what I'd ever remembered hearing. She told me I needed to be born again.

So, on a warm night sometime in June 1971, I knelt down in my tiny apartment and told the Lord that I wanted to be his. At that point, I didn't really understand much about the gospel, but I did understand this: I was desperate, and I desperately believed that the Lord would help me. That prayer on that night changed everything about me. I remember it now, thirty-nine years later, as if it were yesterday.

In the words of Scripture, I knew I needed to be saved, and I trusted that he could save me. One man who came in contact with some of Jesus's followers asked this same question: "What must I do to be saved?" The answer was simple: "Believe in the Lord Jesus, and you will be saved" (Acts 16:31).

Very simply, what do you need to believe in order to be a Christian? You need to know that you need salvation, help, or deliverance. You must not try to reform yourself or decide that you're going to become a moral person so that God will be impressed. Because he is completely holy—that is, perfectly moral—you have to give up any idea that you can be good enough to meet his standard. This is the *good* bad news. It's bad news because it tells you that you're in an impossible situation that you cannot change. But it's also good news because it will free you from endless cycles of self-improvement that end in ultimate failure.

You also need to trust that what you're unable to do—live a perfectly holy life—he's done for you. This is the *good* good news. This is the gospel. Basically, the gospel is the story of how God looked down through the corridors of time and set his love on his people. At a specific point in time, he sent his Son into the world to become fully like us. This is the story you hear about at Christmas. This baby grew to be a man, and after thirty years of obscurity he began to show the people who he was. He did this by performing miracles, healing the sick, and raising the dead. He also demonstrated his deity by teaching people what God required of them, and he continually foretold his coming death and resurrection. And he did one more thing: he claimed to be God.

Because of his claim to be God, the leading religious people, along with the political powers of the day, passed an unjust sentence of death upon him. Although he had never done anything wrong, he was beaten, mocked, and shamefully executed. He died. Even though it looked like he had failed, the truth is that this was God's plan from the very beginning.

His body was taken down from the cross and laid hastily in a rock tomb in a garden. After three days, some of his followers went to go properly care for his remains and discovered that he had risen from the dead. They actually spoke with him, touched him, and ate with him. This is the story that we celebrate at Easter. After another forty days, he was taken back up into heaven, still in his physical form, and his followers were told that he would return to earth in just the same way.

I told you that there are two things you need to know and believe. The first is that you need more significant help than you or any other merely human person could ever supply. The second is that you believe that Jesus, the Christ, is the person who will supply that help and that, if you come to him, he will not turn his back on you. You don't need to understand much more than that, and if you really believe these truths, your life will be transformed by his love.

Below are some verses from the Bible. As you read them, you can talk to God, just as though he were sitting right by you (because his presence is everywhere), and ask him for help to understand.

Remember, his help isn't based on your ability to perfectly understand or on anything that you can do. If you trust him, he's promised to help you, and that's all you need to know for now.

For all have sinned and fall short of the glory of God. (Rom. 3:23)

For the wages of sin is death, but the free gift of God is eternal life in Christ Jesus our Lord. (Rom. 6:23)

For while we were still weak, at the right time Christ died for the ungodly. For one will scarcely die for a righteous person—though perhaps for a good person one would dare even to die—but God shows his love for us in that while we were still sinners, Christ died for us. (Rom. 5:6–8)

For our sake he made him to be sin who knew no sin, so that in him we might become the righteousness of God. (2 Cor. 5:21)

If you confess with your mouth that Jesus is Lord and believe in your heart that God raised him from the dead, you will be saved. For with the heart one believes and is justified, and with the mouth one confesses and is saved. For the Scripture says, "Everyone who believes in him will not be put to shame." . . . The same Lord is Lord of all, bestowing his riches on all who call on him. For "everyone who calls on the name of the Lord will be saved." (Rom. 10:9–13)

Whoever comes to me I will never cast out. (John 6:37)

Therefore, if anyone is in Christ, he is a new creation. The old has passed away; behold, the new has come. (2 Cor. 5:17)

Come to me, all who labor and are heavy laden, and I will give you rest. Take my yoke upon you, and learn from me, for I am gentle and lowly in heart, and you will find rest for your souls. (Matt. 11:28–30)

There is therefore now no condemnation for those who are in Christ Jesus. (Rom. 8:1)

If you'd like to, you might pray a prayer something like this:

Dear God,

I'll admit that I don't understand everything about this, but I do believe these two things: I need help, and you want to help me. I confess that I'm like Elyse and have pretty much ignored you my whole life, except when I was in trouble or just wanted to feel good about myself. I know that I haven't loved you or my neighbor, so it's true that I deserve to be punished and really do need help. But I also believe that you've brought me here, right now, to read this page because you are willing to help me and that if I ask you for help, you won't send me away empty-handed. I'm beginning to understand how you punished your Son in my place and how, because of his sacrifice for me, I can have a relationship with you.

Father, please guide me to a good church and help me understand your Word. I give my life to you and ask you to make me yours.

In Jesus's name, Amen.

Here are two more thoughts. In his kindness, Jesus established his church to encourage and help us to understand and live out these two truths. If you know that you need help and you think that Jesus is able to supply that help, or if you're still questioning but want to know more, please search out a good church in your neighborhood and begin to make relationships there. A good church is one that recognizes that we cannot save ourselves by our own goodness and relies wholly on Jesus Christ (and no one else) for this salvation.

You can call around and ask these questions, or you can even go on the Internet and get a listing of churches in your area. Usually a church's website will have something called a "statement of faith" from which you can get information about the church. Mormon churches (the Church of Jesus Christ of Latter-Day Saints) and those of Jehovah's Witnesses are not Christian churches, and they do not believe in the gospel (though they might tell you they do), so you don't want to go there. Finding a good church is sometimes quite a process, so don't be discouraged if you don't succeed right away. Keep trying and believing that God will help you.

Another factor that will help you grow in this new life of faith is to begin to read what God has said about himself and about us in his Word, the Bible. In the New Testament (the last one-third or so of the

Bible), there are four Gospels or narratives about the life of Jesus. I recommend that you start with the first one, Matthew, and then work your way through the other three. I recommend that you purchase a good modern translation, such as the English Standard Version, but you can get any version (though not a paraphrase) that you're comfortable with and begin reading more right away.

The last request that I have for you is that you contact me through my website, http://www.elysefitzpatrick.com, if you've decided, while reading this book, that you want to follow Jesus.

Thank you for taking time to read this little explanation of the most important news you'll ever hear. You can begin to trust that the Lord will help you understand and become what he wants you to be: a person who's been so loved by him that you're transformed in both your identity and your life.

Notes

1. Martin Luther, *Preface to The Epistle to the Romans* (1552), trans. J. Theodore Mueller (Grand Rapids, MI: Kregel, 1976), *xiii*.
2. The books that I consulted while writing this devotional include: Martin Luther, *The Epistle to the Romans* (1552), trans. J. Theodore Mueller (Grand Rapids, MI: Kregel, 1976); Douglas J. Moo, *The Epistle to the Romans*, New International Commentary on the New Testament (Grand Rapids, MI: Eerdmans, 1996); Leon Morris, *The Epistle to the Romans*, Pillar New Testament Commentary (Grand Rapids, MI: Eerdmans, 1988); John Murray, *The Epistle to the Romans* (Grand Rapids, MI: Eerdmans), 1997; Francis A. Schaeffer, *The Finished Work of Christ: The Truth of Romans 1–8* (Wheaton, IL: Crossway, 1998); R. C. Sproul, *Romans*, St. Andrew's Expositional Commentary (Wheaton, IL: Crossway, 2009); John R. W. Stott, *The Message of Romans*, The Bible Speaks Today (Downers Grove, IL: InterVarsity, 1994).
3. Luther, *Epistle to the Romans*, 37.
4. Stuart Townend, "Loved Before the Dawn of Time (Salvation's Song)," Kingsway Music, 2010.
5. I'm not saying we should sin that grace might abound. I'm saying that even when we do sin, God is mighty enough to garner glory for himself.
6. R. H. Mounce, *Romans*, vol. 27, New American Commentary (Nashville: Broadman, 1995), 102–3.
7. Ibid.
8. Stott, *The Message of Romans*, 109.
9. Quoted in Stott, *The Message of Romans*, 108–9.
10. Quoted in Moo, *The Epistle to the Romans*, 218.
11. Stott, *The Message of Romans*, 109.
12. J. P. Louw and E. A. Nida, *Greek-English Lexicon of the New Testament*, electronic ed. of the 2nd print ed. (New York: United Bible Societies).
13. Iain M. Duguid, *Living in the Gap between Promise and Reality: The Gospel according to Abraham* (Phillipsburg, NJ: P&R, 1999), 56.
14. Speaking of Genesis 15:9–21, "The one who would give the law was here showing that grace comes first, for this was a totally one-sided covenant. It depended entirely on God for its fulfillment. Do you see how amazing this was? God, the ever-living One, was saying, 'I would rather be torn apart than see my relationship with humanity broken, the relationship that I have promised to establish through Abram's descendant.' . . . On the cross, the covenant curse fell completely on Jesus, so that the guilty ones who place their trust in him might experience the blessings of the covenant. Jesus bore the punishment for our sins, so that God might be our God and we might be his people." Duguid, *Living in the Gap*, 59.

Notes

15. Graeme Goldsworthy, *The Goldsworthy Trilogy: Gospel and Kingdom* (Waynesboro, GA: Paternoster, 2000), 112.
16. Note on Genesis 15:6, *ESV Study Bible* (Wheaton, IL: Crossway, 2008).
17. Paul reiterated this thought from the other side of Calvary in his second letter to the Corinthians: "For our sake he made him to be sin who knew no sin, so that in him we might become the righteousness of God" (5:21). Paul scolded the foolish Galatians who were beginning to think that once one was a believer, the way to maintain righteousness was through works: "Does he who supplies the Spirit to you and works miracles among you do so by the works of the law or by hearing with faith—just as Abraham 'believed God, and it was counted to him as righteousness'?" (Gal. 3:5–6).
18. Note on Romans 4:25, *ESV Study Bible*.
19. In our time it's hard to think about our God ever being the kind of God who would execute someone for coming into his presence unbidden or who would bar people from access to his presence, so let me remind you about three other Bible stories, two from the Old Testament and one from the New. The first is the story of Nadab and Abihu, sons of Aaron the priest. God killed them because they went into his presence in an improper way (Lev. 10:1). The second story is that of Uzzah, who had the audacity to put out his hand to steady a cart that the ark of the covenant was being carried on and was killed on the spot (2 Sam. 6:6). The third story is that of Ananias and Sapphira, a husband and wife who lied to the church and thereby lied to God and were struck dead by the Lord (Acts 5:1–11). The ancients, even those in Christ's day, would not have thought that God was like an American senator with an open-door policy.
20. See also Habakkuk 1:13: "You who are of purer eyes than to see evil and cannot look at wrong"; and Psalm 5:5: "The boastful shall not stand before your eyes; you hate all evildoers."
21. Louw and Nida, *Greek-English Lexicon of the New Testament*.
22. Robert Farrar Capon, *Between Noon and Three: Romance, Law, and the Outrage of Grace* (Grand Rapids, MI: Eerdmans, 1997), 96; emphasis original.
23. Louw and Nida, *Greek-English Lexicon of the New Testament*.
24. "Who Mourns for Adonis?" *Star Trek*, season 2, episode 2, September 22, 1967.
25. D. R. W. Wood and I. H. Marshall, *New Bible Dictionary*, 3rd ed. (Downers Grove, IL: InterVarsity, 1996).
26. See also Deuteronomy 9:7; 2 Chronicles 24:18; 34:35; Nahum 1:2–3.
27. Note on Romans 5:10, *ESV Study Bible*.
28. Morris, *Epistle to the Romans*, 237.
29. Charles Wesley, "O For a Thousand Tongues to Sing," ca. 1739.
30. There is some discrepancy as to exactly how old Jesus was when he began his public ministry. Luke says that he was "about thirty" (Luke 3:23), so for ease's sake, that's what we'll go with here.

31. http://wiki.answers.com/Q/How_many_information_bytes_are_processed _by_the_brain_per_second (emphasis added).

32. John Murray, *The Epistle to the Romans* (Grand Rapids, MI: Eerdmans, 1968), 212.

33. Ibid., 213.

34. Of course, the power of our old sin nature is more than a mental imprint, but the analogy is still there.

35. See *ESV Study Bible* note on Romans 6:7. For some reason the word *dikaioo*, which the ESV (and other translations) translates "set free," is in every other occurrence (15 times in Romans, and 25 times in the New Testament) translated "justify." See Stott, *The Message of Romans*, 177.

36. Ibid., 179.

37. I am making an assumption here that my readers have followed Christ into the waters of baptism. It is beyond the scope of this book to discuss what sort of baptism (paedo or believer's). I am simply assuming that you believe that you have been united with Christ in baptism and that your baptism is a sign and seal of that unification. If, on the other hand, you haven't been baptized in a Christian church, then you need to do so right away. Why? Well, first, of course, because you've been commanded to (Matt. 28:19; Acts 2:38; 10:47; 1 Pet. 3:21), and also because you'll need this visible sign to reassure your heart as you embrace your new identity and persevere in faith in your battle against sin.

38. Lewis E. Jones, "There Is Power in the Blood," 1899.

39. Stott, *Message of Romans*, 179.

40. Moo, *Epistle to the Romans*, 387.

41. Stott, *Message of Romans*, 181.

42. Ibid.

43. Murray, *Epistle to the Romans*, 229.

44. Ibid.

45. Note on James 1:14, *ESV Study Bible*.

46. Note on Romans 6:14 in ibid.

47. Murray, *Epistle to the Romans*, 253.

48. Ibid.

49. Corrie ten Boom, *The Hiding Place*, 35th Anniversary Edition (Ada, MI: Chosen, 2006), 228.

Other books by
ELYSE FITZPATRICK

connecting
broken people
**to the love
of Christ**

COUNSEL FROM THE CROSS

Elyse M. Fitzpatrick and
Dennis E. Johnson

FOREWORD BY TULLIAN TCHIVIDJIAN

GIVE THEM
grace

*Dazzling Your Kids
with the Love of Jesus*

Elyse M. Fitzpatrick & Jessica Thompson

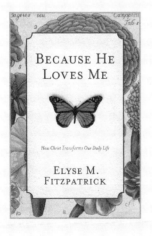

BECAUSE HE
LOVES ME

How Christ Transforms Our Daily Life

ELYSE M.
FITZPATRICK

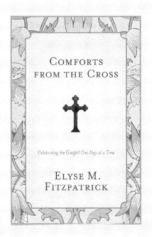

COMFORTS
FROM THE CROSS

Celebrating the Gospel One Day at a Time

ELYSE M.
FITZPATRICK

:: CROSSWAY